MW00467210

Tracing Their Steps

A Memoir

Other works by Bernice Bennett

Our Ancestors, Our Stories

Searching for My South Carolina Kin

**Reverend Peter Clark (seated) and his son Moses Clark, circa 1906.
From the Bernice Bennett Collection.**

Tracing Their Steps

A Memoir

by Bernice Alexander Bennett

My Journey to Find Granddaddy's Land in Livingston Parish, Louisiana

Palmyra, VA
Shortwood Press
2019

Front cover: "Our Little Old Church" (Oil on canvas)
©2003, 2019 Ted Ellis. Used with permission.

Edited and formatted by Jean L. Cooper.

ISBN-13: 978-1-7336484-0-0
ISBN-10: 1-7336484-0-2

Dedication

I dedicate this book to my Grandmother
Rebecca Watson Mitchell (MaBecky)

and to my Mother, Bernice Mitchell Alexander

Table of Contents

Acknowledgments

I would like to express my gratitude to the many colleagues and friends that listen to my endless stories about the search for my great-great-grandfather Peter Clark's land.

Special thanks go to Clark Forrest, Jeff Boyd, Antoinette Harrell, Iris Stilley, Stephanie Martin Quiette, Judy Riffel, and Leonard Smith, III, for directing me to important resources in Louisiana.

In addition, I am indebted and appreciate my accountability partner Christine Easterling and Write Your Life coach Anita R. Henderson for pushing and encouraging me to tell my story. I am also thankful to Angela Walton-Raji, Patricia Glover Howard, Shelley Murphy, Ellen Butler, Kathy Marshall, and Janice Woods for providing constructive feedback concerning this book.

I further acknowledge the support of my husband, Glen Bennett, and my adult children, Denise and Dwight Bennett, and granddaughter Anika Bennett for encouraging me to write this family story.

Foreword

This book addresses a need in the historiography of Livingston Parish, Louisiana, namely, the need for an extensive history of the parish's African-American citizens. Bennett is well suited for this task since she is an accomplished family historian and genealogist with research experience extending from the Florida Parishes to the National Archives in Washington, DC. She writes with the flair of a novelist, but the facts and events she recounts are real.

This is a story that has taken a long time to be told: How African-Americans in the Deep South survived the Civil War to become landowners, only, in the case of Bennett's family, to lose that accomplishment and dream.

This story is a microcosm of the national migration pattern that many African-Americans took from the farm to the city. Bennett's ancestors moved from St. Helena Parish, Louisiana to south Livingston and then to New Orleans. From there, they stayed in contact with the family members who remained in the parish.

Everyone should read Bennett's story with an interest in and love of history. It is an American story, and she is exploring how African Americans in Livingston Parish came together to own land under the Homestead Act of 1862. You will have to read this book to learn more about how Peter Clark homesteaded his land and helped his neighbors to do the same.

Clark Forrest
President, Edward Livingston Historical Association

Key Names

Rebecca Watson Mitchell (1894–2000), **MaBecky** (Becky or Rebecca)—My maternal grandmother.

Isabella Clark Watson Skinner Harris (1879–1955) (Mama Isabella, Sista Isabella)—My maternal great-grandmother, mother of Rebecca Watson Mitchell, grandmother of Bernice Mitchell Alexander.

Peter Clark (1855–1909)—My maternal great-great-grandfather, father of Isabella Clark Watson Skinner Harris, and grandfather of Rebecca Watson Mitchell.

Rebecca Youngblood Clark (1860–1900)—My maternal great-great-grandmother, wife of Peter Clark, mother of Isabella Clark Watson Skinner Harris, grandmother of Rebecca Watson Mitchell.

Thomas Youngblood (1835–1882)—My 3x great-grandfather and father of Rebecca Youngblood Clark, father-in-law of Peter Clark, grandfather of Isabella Clark Watson Skinner Harris, great-grandfather of Rebecca Watson Mitchell.

Minerva Smith Youngblood (1835–1879)—My 3x great-grandmother and wife of Thomas Youngblood, mother of Rebecca Youngblood Clark, mother-in-law of Peter Clark, grandmother of Isabella Clark Watson Skinner Harris, great-grandmother of Rebecca Watson Mitchell.

Bernice Mitchell Alexander (1914–2010)—My mother, daughter of Rebecca Watson Mitchell, granddaughter of Isabella Clark Watson Skinner Harris, great-granddaughter of Peter Clark and Rebecca Youngblood Clark, 2x great-granddaughter of Thomas Youngblood and Minerva Smith Youngblood.

Henry Ernest Watson (1876 –Unknown)—My great-grandfather, first husband of Isabella (Clark) Watson Skinner Harris and father of Rebecca (Watson) Mitchell.

Bernice Mitchell Alexander - Maternal Family Tree

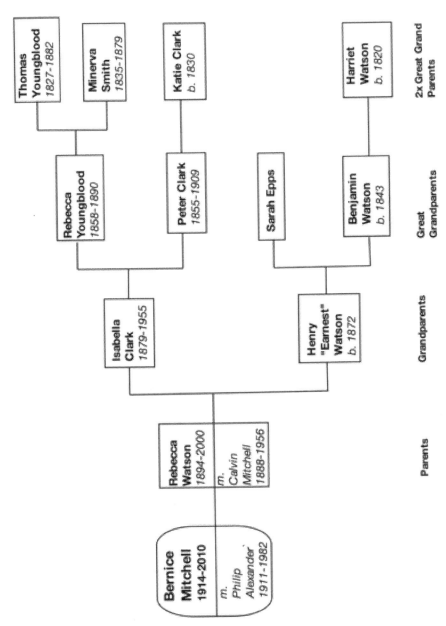

Thomas Youngblood
1827-1882

Minerva Smith
1835-1879

Katie Clark
b. 1830

Harriet Watson
b. 1820

2x Great Grand Parents

Rebecca Youngblood
1858-1890

Peter Clark
1855-1909

Sarah Epps

Benjamin Watson
b. 1843

Great Grandparents

Isabella Clark
1879-1955

Henry "Earnest" Watson
b. 1872

Grandparents

Rebecca Watson
1894-2000
m.
Calvin Mitchell
1888-1956

Parents

Bernice Mitchell
1914-2010
m.
Philip Alexander
1911-1982

Introduction:
Visiting MaBecky

Many years ago, I could not wait to visit my grandmother MaBecky—Rebecca was her real name. MaBecky's beautiful soft cocoa-brown skin was the envy of all of us because in spite of her age, she had few wrinkles that would give any hints that she was over 100 years old. I admired her gentle demeanor of peace and calmness and found her willing to share what she could about the family history. She always had something good to say about her life and about living and was there for her grandchildren and family. All my childhood friends knew my grandmother.

She called me Laine, short for Elaine—my middle name. I don't think that I ever heard her call me Bernice.

Her modest one-bedroom senior citizen's apartment on the second floor in Gordon Plaza in the upper ninth ward of New Orleans was decorated with family photos and a tapestry with colonial scenes of old New Orleans. Her green brocade French provincial sofa was adorned with pillows and crocheted doilies she had painstakingly made on one of her craft days at the Senior Citizens Center.

At 100 years old, MaBecky was still living by herself, even though she used a walking stick to get around. She complained a little about Arthur (you know—Arthritis), but it did not stop her from doing what she wanted to do around her "little place" and her community. After cataract surgery, MaBecky marveled at how well she could see and commented on seeing small wrinkles on her hands that she had not noticed before the surgery. She had high blood pressure and never had a problem remembering to take her "pressure pills."

Upon walking into her apartment, I immediately smelled her seafood gumbo with a hint of spices consisting of creole seasoning and the trinity—bell peppers, onions, and celery. This was gumbo heaven, and MaBecky could definitely cook the traditional creole dishes of New Orleans. If you could taste her stewed chicken you would want to lick the bowl. In fact, the chicken was so good that after you finished eating the meat you would chew on the bone.

In her small living room she had her table ready with two chairs, and one was waiting for me. Two round and deep gumbo bowls were on that table, big enough to handle all the ingredients (chicken, shrimp, crab, sausage, and oysters). No hot dogs or corn were added to this mixture. She had everything ready for our meal including Leidenheimer French Bread from the Bakery on Simon Bolivar and Thalia Streets. Well, let's just say that my taste buds were on overdrive and salivating. And I was ready to eat. Also, she had Zatarain's Gumbo File powder just in case I needed to add a little more spice to my dish.

But I did resist sitting down at the table and scanned the living room before we ate to admire the "whatnots" and other items my grandmother had around her apartment. Lord knows that was hard to do when the familiar aroma of creole cooking was calling me to eat.

In front of her sofa was a brown coffee table full of a little bit of everything. Her Bible, the *Louisiana Weekly,* and the *New Orleans Data News Weekly*—every Black household had copies of the Black newspapers from New Orleans as well as *Jet* and *Ebony* magazines. I noticed a photo album, the kind of album with the sticky back and clear plastic on each page. Most of the photos were stuck on the pages with glue. Because of age, the plastic covering had slipped around in the book, with some pages not having any plastic at all.

Nevertheless, this photo album would open up a memory that could have been lost forever, because no one was interested enough or willing to sit down to look at it. Not me. I wanted to see every photo and hear the stories that came with them.

So, after eating two heaping bowls of gumbo, I settled on that green sofa right next to MaBecky and waited to hear the story. Of course, I had my questions. Sometimes I knew the answers, but I just enjoyed talking to her. Her smile was infectious, and her false teeth gave her a youthful appearance along with her smooth cocoa-brown skin and long white hair with blue rinse that prevented the gray from turning her hair yellow. MaBecky unrolled her pink plastic curlers to show me how long her hair had grown. I touched it, and it was soft like cotton. She always had a warm straightening comb to smooth out her curly hair. Although she really did not need to do this.

A friend asked me if my grandmother knew any former slaves, or were any of her grandparents enslaved? So I asked my grandmother. She looked in my eyes, and a serious look came over her face when she said, "No." Not just *NO*, but a long *NOOOOO*. Her body stiffened, and I could tell that I may have touched on a sensitive issue.

However, she had more important information to tell me. But we first had to look at the photos in the album. She slowly turned the pages to an old picture and began to stroke the photo.

"This is my granddaddy Peter Clark, with Uncle Moses, and my granddaddy owned a lot of land in Maurepas, Louisiana."

The loving look on her face and the softness in her voice made me realize that she was sharing something very important with me. She was smiling and sat up straight and proud. I immediately felt a kinship to him because of how MaBecky's voice changed as she began to speak slowly, saying her granddaddy's name—Peter Clark.

I heard more. MaBecky was born in Maurepas, in 1894. Her grandfather Peter Clark and her grandmother Rebecca (Youngblood) Clark resided in St. Helena and Livingston Parishes.

With a big smile, MaBecky said that she was named after her

maternal grandmother, Rebecca (Youngblood) Clark. I could not believe what I was hearing. To get my maternal twice-great-grandparents' names—Peter Clark and Rebecca (Youngblood) Clark—well, that was a special gift. She just gave me those names through a simple matter-of-fact conversation. I didn't have to work or probe for those names—just listen. The power of oral history has revealed so much to me, and I was fixated on what I had just been told.

From previous conversations I knew that my grandmother's father's name was Ernest Watson. I never saw a photo of him in my life. Rumor had it that he just disappeared without a trace. My maternal great-grandmother—MaBecky's mother, Isabella (Clark) Watson Skinner Harris—married again after her first husband vanished.

After about five hours, MaBecky began to clean up her little place and put on her blue cotton bathrobe. This signaled to me that she was ready to head to bed. I also needed to go back home to my mother's house. Yes, five hours and it only felt like a few minutes.

But before I left the apartment, MaBecky gave me the only known photo of her grandfather. And on the back of that photo she wrote "Reverend Peter Clark and Uncle Moses." I wanted to cry! Instead I gave her a big hug and promised to cherish that photo forever and find Peter Clark's land.

I knew one day that I would also share the story about how my twice-great-grandfather owned a lot of land, with my children, grandchildren, and others.

This story will show the many twists and turns I encountered in the search to find the land that my grandmother MaBecky knew existed. My journey is described in this book, *Tracing Their Steps*.

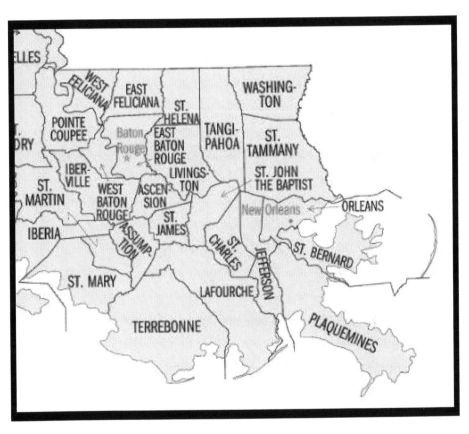

Map of Southeastern Louisiana.
US Census Bureau.

Chapter 1
Let the Journey Begin

I was not sure how I should tackle the promise I made to my grandmother. I kept the photo of Peter Clark in a safe place to share with as many family members as possible. However, finding information on the land could be a challenge.

Therefore, with just basic information, I set out to verify the oral history and find the dirt. My mother's eagerness to find the property also pushed me with encouraging words to move forward in my research. She promised "to help me in any way possible." But we needed a plan to find Peter Clark in written documents.

My mother stayed in touch with family members all over the United States, and if anybody could help me find information, it was Mama. And she did just that. She pulled out her little green phone book that looked more like a diary. It had names, phone numbers, and addresses, and noted whether the individuals were dead or alive. She was certain that a relative in Covington, Louisiana, could track down the old family Bible with Peter Clark's name in it.

MaBecky moved into Mama's house when she was around 102 years old and enjoyed the attention as people marveled at her longevity and wit. I framed one of the many certificates she received from former

Mayor Marc Morial when she turned 102 years old. In addition, she received a Happy Birthday letter from President Clinton and showed it off to family and friends.

On December of 1999, the WWL-TV Action News reporter in New Orleans came to discuss services available for Caregivers of Aging Parents. I'll never forget the video of that show when my mother told the reporter to ask her, "How does it feel to be 105 years old?" With a broad smile and a little chuckle, my grandmother said, "I like being that age. I think that this is a good age."

I often play that videotape just to see MaBecky once again getting her long white hair combed by the Senior Attendant and hearing the rhythmic cadence of each word in her New Orleans accent.

I got off-track with my research after my grandmother passed in 2000, a few days before her 106th birthday. Job and family responsibilities became my priority.

However, in 2004, I began a search for my father's family in Ninety-Six and Edgefield, South Carolina. This journey led to a miraculous connection with my South Carolina Kemp/Frazier cousins. We found descendants of our great-great-grandfather, Andrew Kemp, who was enslaved by Henry Johnson Kemp in Edgefield. In addition, we connected with Henry Johnson Kemp's descendant.

Although my mother was happy to see me make those family connections on my paternal side, she also wanted me to get back to my search for Peter Clark's land.

Chapter 2
The Life-Changing Event

Mama began to share with family and non-family members that I was searching for information about Peter Clark. To my surprise, during a visit to New Orleans in May of 2005, a large brown box was sitting on my mother's dining-room table. In that box, wrapped in a black plastic bag was a big, old, black Bible. Mama had located the family Bible in the possession of an in-law of her late great-aunt Martha Callahan. This in-law was located in Covington, Louisiana. Her great-aunt Martha was the sister of my mother's grandmother, Isabella (Clark) Harris. Mama's former minister, Reverend Walter B. Pennington of Grace United Methodist Church in New Orleans, had picked it up for her because he lived there.

It was obvious that my mother had talked to several relatives about the Bible, and I expected to see a small Bible that folks took to church. It was hard to believe that after all these years she managed to get the Bible and that it had not been thrown away.

I was overwhelmed and physically shaking when I saw that Bible because I never knew that it truly existed. But Mama knew. This is one of many clues she would offer me in my journey to find Peter Clark's land.

Taking a deep breath, I slowly lifted the black leather-covered

Bible with the words *"Holy Bible"* engraved on the front cover. I did not know what I would find.

I opened each page, trying to take in all the emotions, fearing that the old and fragile pages would crumble. Realizing that my twice-great-grandfather's name could be in that Bible gave me hope. I felt like a kid opening a Christmas present—anxious and excited. Yet, I had to be patient because I did not want to damage the book by ripping through the pages.

The Bible's cover page had big letters—*Self-Pronouncing Edition—Combination—Holy Bible containing The Old and New Testaments. Translated out of the Original Tongues.*

The International Publishing Company of Philadelphia, Pennsylvania, published this book in 1895. Now, according to my grandmother, she was born in 1894. I knew that Peter Clark was born much earlier than the publication date on this book. Nevertheless, this Bible could include information about family events.

I went beyond the various scriptures to Family Records in the middle page of the Bible. This page listed Dates of Births, Dates of Marriages, and Dates of Deaths. Additional pages included Holy Matrimony, Deaths, and Memorandum, and even had a page for Family Temperance Pledge.

Perhaps many households back in the day had large Bibles like this one?

Each entry in the Bible appeared to be written as a diary. Little comments like, "My good friend Mary died today," or a bank entry documenting a monetary deposit, and information about events in the community.

And then I saw it in black-and-white—Peter Clark's birth date, January 31, 1855, and the date of his death, May 22, 1909. That entry took my breath away. I called out,

"Mama, look! Look! Peter Clark's name is in the Bible."

She already knew this but was smiling with pride because she helped me find the first document to verify that Peter Clark had existed.

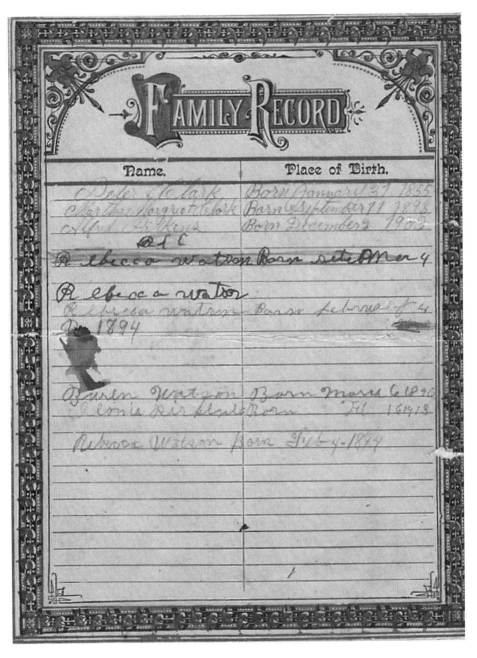

Family Record from the Clark Family Bible

29

Peter's name is not the only name of significance in this Bible. My grandmother's name is also in the Bible—Rebecca Watson, born March 4, 1894, and another birth entry, February 4, 1894. The recorder of this information was unsure about the exact date of my grandmother's birth, and MaBecky always told the family that her birth date was February 4, 1894. Her brother is also in the Bible—Burlen Watson, born March 6, 1896—as is the birth date (September 11, 1898) of Margaret Clark, my great-grandmother Isabella's sister, and on and on. Many other names are in the Bible, but they had no meaning to me at the time. Those names would become significant as I continued my journey in search of my twice-great-grandfather's land.

Peter's birth year of 1855 did show that he was born during slavery time. Although Peter's granddaughter, my grandmother MaBecky, never offered information that her grandfather was enslaved, he was born during a period when he and his family were most likely slaves. However, as with any journey, I had to find more documents to verify his life as far back as possible.

I could see that someone was clearly recording information as family members were born and died. However, the entries in the Bible were in different handwritings, and some written by pen and others in pencil.

The most amazing discovery in this Bible was a small envelope with a 4-cent stamp containing a letter written on July 30, 1961, by my grandmother to her Aunt Martha Callahan, her mother's sister, at Box 121, Covington, Louisiana. This letter was in pristine condition and tucked between the scriptures.

My grandmother's voice in that letter to her Aunt Martha indicated that the Bible entry could serve as evidence for her to apply for the old age pension.

Transcript of the letter as written:

2124 Thalia Street
New Orleans, La.
July 30, 1961

My Dear Aunt

Just a few lines to let you here from me all is well hope when you receive this letter it will find you well. I think you should come and get this Bible with your age in it so you can get your social security you are old enough to start drawing it now do you know how old you are now you are 63 years old and you have mist one year because you should have started at 62 if the Bible was so big I could mail it to you but it is so large you can call me sometime and let me know when you are coming to get it call me sometime my number 5231758 call me if you don't write how is all your children and where are they all is you working yet if you have a phone send me your number so I can call you sometime how can you stay so close and don't write a word. I will close.

From your niece
Rebecca Mitchell
2124 Thalia St New Orleans 13 LA.[1]

---

[1] Bernice Bennett has the original letter discovered in 2005 in the family Bible.

Martha Callahan.
Photo courtesy of her son, Joseph Callahan.

Martha Callahan's son Joseph (Peter Clark's grandson), whom I met for the first time in 2017, sent me a photo of his mother. He was unaware of the letter I'd found but could verify where his mother was living in 1961. She died in 1963, and we both hoped that my grandmother had been able to see her aunt before she passed away.

Chapter 3
Making Sense

Recreating events in Peter's life from his birth in 1855 and death in 1909 was part of my journey to find the land. Since Peter Clark died in 1909, finding a death certificate or some other written document could confirm the accuracy of the death year as stated in the Bible.

Ordering Peter Clark's death certificate from the Louisiana State Archives in Baton Rouge was easy. I only waited a couple of weeks, and there in black-and-white I saw his name. Peter Clark died of tuberculosis at Charity Hospital in New Orleans on May 22, 1909.[2] He was fifty-five years old and from Maurepas. My grandmother told me that she had lived there, and now I had the first verifiable document with evidence that Peter was from that mysterious place with the French-sounding name.

I did not just stop at obtaining the death certificate and also searched for a newspaper entry of his death. So far, I could not find that information.

But—wait a minute—could that be Peter Clark? Yes, I did find a

---

[2] Peter Clark, Certificate of Death, State of Louisiana, Secretary of State, Division of Archives, Orleans Death Indices, 1909-1917, vol.146, p.874.

May 25, 1909, newspaper entry in the *Times Picayune* listing deaths during that time period. Peter Clark's name is there!

With this information, I had the parameters to begin the search for Peter's land, between 1870 and 1909. Anytime earlier and he would have been too young to have purchased land. And any time after 1909, he was dead.

I mailed the Bible and other old family papers to my home in Maryland. I also took a picture of a portrait of my great-grandmother Isabella, MaBecky's mother, that hung on the wall in my mother's home.

It had to be fate that drew me back to MaBecky's story and my promise to find Peter Clark's property. Within a matter of months, everything that was precious about going home to New Orleans was destroyed by the floodwaters of Hurricane Katrina in August of 2005. This was a tragedy for New Orleans and also the entire country. Everyone around the world was fixated on the extent of damage and lives destroyed during this time period.

That's right. I was in New Orleans in May, shipped the Bible and other family papers to Maryland. If I had not removed those items, they would have been gone forever. Just putting this in writing is bringing me to tears. My head and eyes hurt from lack of sleep as I struggled to figure out what I could do to help my family. Twelve hours of weather reports about the approaching hurricane left me in a helpless state of anxiety.

Frantic phone calls every thirty minutes to my sisters, brother, and mother was all I could do to make certain that they were packed and heading out of New Orleans. They needed to leave before the eye of storm came barreling down with the wind and rain. I prayed, "Heavenly father, please protect my family."

Before evacuating from mother's house, my sister removed the photos from the wall and put them in plastic bags. She thought that at least some of the family mementoes might be saved if the area flooded.

Thanks to my sister Cynthia, the family crowded into one car and headed out of town to Bossier City, Louisiana. They (mother, brother, sisters, and niece) all expected to return home later the following week and took few possessions with them.

However, because of a levee break, massive flooding engulfed the city, and everyone experienced a loss. Mama's house was encased with festering murky floodwater, and the interior of her house had black mold growing on the walls and carpet. Both sisters also had major flood damage to their homes.

In the meantime, my house in Maryland became the temporary sanctuary for my mother, brother, and niece. My twin sister Janice moved to Memphis to be near her children, and Cynthia remained in Baton Rouge. She just could not move away from New Orleans—the City that she loved. It was too emotional, with so many memories...

Getting back to my research gave me the opportunity to involve my Mother even more in assisting me. It was also therapeutic for her to witness my progress as I gathered information on Peter Clark.

One day I surprised my mother with a copy of her grandmother Mama Isabella's portrait, the portrait that she thought she would never see again. She also had a small photo of her grandmother that she took around 1940, and I enlarged and framed that photo for her.

My Mother continued to live with me until my sisters and I worked out an arrangement where she would stay with all three of us. This arrangement worked out well because my Mother—"the Social Butterfly"—loved meeting new people. She joined the Senior Citizens group near my house and made new friends and taught them how to quilt. When she went to Memphis, she joined a Senior Citizens group there, and when she returned to New Orleans (my sister had completed the construction of her new home in New Orleans) Mama reconnected with her old friends and church family.

When Mama lived with me she also acquired a research card from the National Archives in Washington, D.C. I now carry that card with me everywhere I go for good luck.

Since Mama was back in New Orleans on one of her rotational trips, she wanted me to visit Maurepas. She felt that seeing the location would help and motivate me to continue my search for the land.

Chapter 4
Visiting the Homeplace

Mama wanted to get on the highway early in the morning! However, I was tired—crazy, lazy tired after flying into New Orleans from Maryland, and just wanted to sleep.

Sleep was not going to happen for me! I had to get up, pick up the rental car, and get on I-10 in Louisiana heading west before the heavy traffic could prevent us from getting to the little town called Killian—in the country. Yes, the country, a small rural town in Livingston Parish. I just did not know if I could take that ride across and over the swamps! It would only take about ninety minutes, but I was tired.

However, I knew that Mama would talk through the entire drive, and she did!

I heard more stories about growing up in Louisiana and realized that I had a history to love and embrace. After all I needed to hear those stories to share with my own adult children and grandchild.

So, up and on my way! Bottled water, bananas, apples, a full tank of gas, sunglasses, and we would arrive in the Florida Parishes sooner than I could imagine.

Mama is the navigator, and at ninety years old she knew every exit and shortcut to that special place called home.

Oh no! She forgot her Butterfly pin. Should I turn around?

The blue rays from the sun shone as we began our trip to Livingston Parish. Maurepas is in the south/southwestern area of Livingston Parish, and it is also known as Head of Island or Whitehall. The area of Maurepas is located along the Livingston Parish/Ascension Parish line.[3]

The day was perfect. No rain, little humidity, and a light breeze—this is the Louisiana summer weather that I was hoping for. It seemed like an unknown force was clearing the way for us to have a travel-free ride. When I say travel-free, I mean no major backups heading to the airport, nothing stopping us on the I-10 highway, and well, just the perfect day!

Mama was giddy and talkative like a schoolgirl. Oh yes, she did have her purple and green iridescent Butterfly pin. The one she bought at the flea market—just a piece of cheap costume jewelry, but it was a butterfly. I called it her good luck jewelry. I don't know why she had to put on that particular pin because she had a lot of them. She just loved her pins. She said that it represented how life changes over time and that we should always remember that a butterfly is—well—she stopped dead in her conversation and stared into the distance.

I could tell that she was thinking about all the experiences in her life, so I allowed her to go inside herself for a moment of reflection.

Okay, we were inching to the right lane to exit the I-10 highway toward Highway 55, Highway 12, and then Highway 22. I saw the tree stumps in the water and the heat waves swirling in front of me with the bright sunlight shining over lanes of that serene bridge.

This is a drive that is either exhilarating or boring. It's so quiet and still. I could see the pale green algae covering swampy water, and I was just waiting for an alligator to take a lazy walk on the bridge. After all, who would care? Not a lot of traffic and the alligator would have the right of way.

Glancing in my rearview mirror, I saw a big eighteen-wheeler coming fast behind me without a care in the world. Mama was just

---

[3] https://en.wikipedia.org/wiki/Maurepas,_Louisiana

talking and talking. I heard her say something about her daddy, Calvin Mitchell.

"Your Daddy did what?"

"Oh," she said, "it would take my Daddy two days to get here in the old days."

"Well, how did he get to New Orleans?"

"By train and sometimes boat."

Mama was just talking and talking. I could hear sound, but my mind drifted because the scenery was hypnotizing.

I glanced slightly to my right again and asked, "Mama, what are you talking about?"

"Oh, I am just happy to take this trip." She pointed. "Look at those tree stumps. The Indians would never have destroyed this land. Yes, and look at those birds in the water—they are so graceful gliding low to catch a fish, maybe a shrimp, crawfish—who knows? Well, this is their habitat! Sure is, and they are surviving and thriving in spite of what man has done to destroy everything."

"But it is pretty, Mama," I said, looking at the grey Spanish moss hanging on the trees.

"Yes, it is."

"Mama, what do you remember about coming to New Orleans as a child?"

Chapter 5
Mama's Childhood Memories

"You see, back in the olden times, colored children did not attend school as long as the white kids did. Maybe two to three months and that was it. My grandmother Isabella did not want that for me because education was important. And that was the end of her discussion about my education. I was off to school in Madisonville, where my Uncle Will (my grandmother's brother) lived before moving to New Orleans to attend Thomy Lafon Elementary School, and John McDonogh 35 Senior High School." McDonogh 35 was the first high school in the state of Louisiana for African-American students.

Mama continued, "You know Aunt Hester (Mama Isabella's sister) had already moved from Livingston Parish to New Orleans with my cousins Josephine, Minerva, Augustine, and Pinkie. I was so happy to be around them."

"What did your daddy have to say about you leaving Livingston Parish?"

"Mama was okay with it, and I was always going back to see my daddy's mother Grandma Tish (Lutesia), Grandpa Ben, Aunt Lizzie, and all the other family members, so it was okay with them."

"Tell me about living in the country?"

Mama said, "I was born in Clio, a little town near Maurepas and Killian. Not much there, just woods, mosquitoes, and water. My daddy pulled boats. He later bought property in Killian, in 1918, down the street from Grandpa Ben's land that he bought in 1888."

"You know, the Mitchells were kind of prominent because they owned land. My Grandma Tish was a smart old lady. Grandpa Ben married her in Raymond, Hinds County, Mississippi, and brought her back to Louisiana. Grandma Tish wanted a house with a parlor just like the house where she was raised in Mississippi."

"Mama, what do you mean?"

"I mean that some white people in Raymond, Mississippi, raised my Grandma Tish, and she expected Grandpa Ben to keep her in the type of house she was accustomed to. Oh, I do remember that house with a shiny tin roof, parlor, the porch, and water well. I also remembered Grandpa Ben as a light-complexioned man that spoke with a French accent. I thought that his wife was Ms. Nancy. Ms. Nancy was his second wife after Grandma Tish died in the early 1940s.

"Family members use to call me little Calvin after my daddy, and others said that I resembled my Grandma Tish."

While I listened to this flood of information, Mama continued, "Did I tell you that my Grandma Tish was a smart old lady? She knew about farming and would make those sons help her plow the land. It was a beautiful sight to see all those rows of vegetables, greens, beans, cabbage, and sweet potatoes. We would dig holes and put the potatoes once harvested in a bank."

"Mama, I don't know what you are talking about—a bank?"

"Well, this was what they called it. We could store the potatoes in the soil and dig them up whenever we wanted to cook and eat them."

"Since, you are talking about food, what did you eat every day?"

"We ate chicken and fish, fresh vegetables—lots of greens and beans, sweet potatoes, fresh milk and buttermilk, cornbread, and very little meat. Maybe once in a while someone would kill a hog."

"Did you eat any beef?"

"Not much."

But Mama was laughing and enjoying the conversation. "One day," she said, "my brothers and I went to the creek to find some crawfish—my mama"—my grandmother MaBecky—"called them mudbugs. We would put a piece of meat on a stick and swirl it in the water for the crawfish to latch on, and leave with a big can full of mudbugs. We put salt on them when they were alive to clean them out, rinse off the salt, and boil them. That was a fun time for me!"

"What else did you do during your childhood?"

Mama continued on, "I loved going to Sunday School. My daddy had an old buggy with a horse named Ted. I just loved taking that ride to church."

We finally arrived in Killian and stopped at our Cousin Lillie Mae's house. Lillie Mae is a Youngblood descendant. Her husband, W.A., accompanied us to Maurepas. This was a trip down memory lane for Mama. For me, this was an adventure to see a place that I had heard of but did not know a lot about.

Maurepas was close to my mother's birthplace—a quick ten-minute drive from Clio.

It is a small rural town—nothing special to see. It was settled and occupied by people of French, German, and Spanish ancestry. I knew that my great-grandpa Ben Mitchell's birthplace (Ben was my grandfather Calvin Mitchell's father) was born in French Settlement.

I had never put all the pieces together until this trip to realize that my family settled in a place that must have had some historical context for the African-American presence there. I just needed to figure that out. How did my family get there? Were they free or enslaved? Did they always live in that part of Louisiana?

A man named Pierre LeBourgeois[4] acquired land from John McDonogh, a shipping merchant. This is the area where that land was located. I could only speculate that maybe my ancestors were associated

---

[4] Pardue, D. N. "Biography of Pierre Etienne LeBourgeois, Livingston, St. James and Orleans Parishes, Louisiana." *French Settlement Historical Register*, v. 5 (December 1980). French Historical Society. http://files.usgwarchives.net/la/orleans/bios/l-000014.txt.

with Le Bourgeois' land.

We visited the Goodwill Cemetery on Head of Island where my Youngblood family members were all buried and also the family-owned Mitchell Cemetery in Killian. But we did not find the final resting place of Peter Clark.

Chapter 6
Life in Livingston Parish for African Americans

Whenever I spoke to my cousins about Livingston Parish, they never had anything positive to say about it. I heard a lot about the violence and racial tension in this Parish.

My grandmother, on the other hand, spoke with a faraway look, smiled and behaved as if it was the best place to live. Surrounded by family and growing up when her granddaddy owned a lot of land might have protected her from the evils of the community.

As a little girl, she attended Tiger Bluff Baptist Church School. I found a photo in the dresser drawer in Mama's house prior to Hurricane Katrina that included MaBecky with about twenty children and three teachers. Some of the children were kneeling while others appear to stand at attention. I envisioned each child walking through the piney woods in bare feet to avoid getting their shoes dirty and being told, "Don't move," as they waited for the photographer to capture that once-in-a-lifetime photo.

MaBecky as a little girl is in that photo, standing erect next to her teacher Miss Delphine. Her hair is combed neatly with two braids, and she is wearing a dress. All three of the teachers are in long skirts and high-necked Victorian white blouses, with neatly coifed hair. I think that my grandmother was about six years old then. She looked about that young in the photo. Perhaps these teachers were Jeanes teachers[5] who worked in the rural South setting up schools in old churches and cabins, or perhaps in the piney woods of Livingston Parish.

Speaking of the piney woods, I saw trucks hauling lumber on the highway. The timber industry must be a major economic base for this community. With that said, I could clearly understand why my grandmother talked about the land.

Little has been written about the history of the African-American presence or contribution to the community there.

The history of Livingston Parish did reveal that "under 20% of the households owned slaves and slaves comprised about 28.5% of the total population. In 1860, Livingston ranked second with the fewest number of slaves of any parish with 1,171."[6] Nevertheless, in my mind, one person in bondage is too many for me.

Yet, even with these statistics, I wanted to know where the plantations were located.

Voter registration and voting in general created an uproar during 1876 election season in Livingston Parish. African-American voters and individuals supportive of the Republican party endured intimidation and violence by armed men identified as the "buckshot and coal-oil clan or regulators." On November 28, 1876, a number of witnesses were called before the Commissioner of the United States Circuit Court to testify concerning the election. The eyewitness testimony illustrated the difficult life the African-American community experienced in

---

[5] http://education.stateuniversity.com/pages/2135/Jeanes-Teachers.html

[6] "The Civil War Years," in *The History of Livingston Parish, Louisiana.* Compiled and edited by the History Committee—Edward Livingston Historical Association. Gateway Press, 1986, C7, p.21.

Livingston Parish during Reconstruction.[7] For example, I read that "William Foster, a colored schoolteacher in the sixth ward, was assaulted by a mob a few days before the election being pelted with eggs and receiving death threats. This violence broke up the school."

---

[7] 1876 Congressional Investigation - Vote for Electors in Louisiana – Livingston Parish, p. 483- 511.

Chapter 7
Tracing Through Records

Since Peter Clark died in 1909, I looked for him in other events in the early 1900s. I discovered in that pile of papers I took from Mama's house a pristine receipt documenting the loan of $80.00 by Octave LeBourgeois to Peter Clark, on January 16, 1904, in Maurepas. The

IOU from Peter Clark to Octave LeBourgeois for the loan of $80 in 1904.

interest rate of $8 was payable at White Hall, Louisiana , and signed by

Peter (his mark) Clark. The loan was payable in one year, on January 16, 1905. Peter complied by making monthly cash payments and writing on the back of the receipt each time he paid on his debt. I wondered if Octave LeBourgeois and Pierre Etienne LeBourgeois who negotiated with John McDonogh for land could have been related to each other?

Searching in the US Census

In the 1900 US census, Peter Clark is living in Maurepas, with his wife Violla Clark, and children William Clark, Mary Clark, and Martha Clark, and grandchildren Becky Clark and Berlin Clark.

My grandmother Becky and her brother are listed with the Clark surname. But where was my great-grandmother Isabella, and why was my grandmother listed as a Clark? An even bigger surprise was to see a woman named Violla Clark who had been married to Peter for about nine years. What happened to Rebecca Youngblood Clark? Could Rebecca and Violla be the same person? Did the census taker visit the house? Did someone in the neighborhood provide information about the Clark family?

In further exploring this record, Peter is 41 years old with a birth year of 1859. Shrugging my shoulders and thinking out loud, "I guess he was getting younger."

However, the most exciting entry on the census was Peter Clark's occupation—a farmer and owner of his own land, free and clear. He could read, write, and speak English.

Ok, this was a happy dance moment for me—just a little shake and movement with my head and snap of my fingers while hearing my internal music playing "Oh Happy Days!"

I wondered why my grandmother Rebecca or Becky was listed in the census as Clark rather than Watson? She did appear in the household with her granddaddy and most likely celebrated with her aunts and uncles when her granddaddy acquired his land. She understood that owning this brown dirt was a significant achievement to share with her descendants.

One of Peter's neighbors on the 1900 US Census was Octave

LeBourgeois, and he also owned land. Perhaps they were just friends, or maybe Octave was just willing to offer him a helping hand, even if he did charge 8 percent interest on the loan.

The 1900 US Census provided me with just what I needed—verification that Peter Clark owned property. But it did not tell me when and how he acquired it.

If I looked in 1880 US Census, I would miss twenty years of information on Peter's life. So, I took a chance and searched old newspapers to see what I might find. Just maybe his name would be in the newspaper.

Chapter 8
Discovering the Unthinkable

Oh no! Peter Clark's name was in the newspaper, but it was because of a tragedy. A story in The *Maurepas Gazette* on March 14, 1884, described how my twice-great-uncle Louis Youngblood (Rebecca Youngblood's brother) came to his death at the hands of his brother Thomas Youngblood. This is one of those times where I wished that I had not found this information. The headline was *"Murder in Livingston Parish."* Shaking my head with disbelief, I slowly read the details of this murder.

Last Tuesday night the notorious hoodlum Tom Youngblood shot and killed his brother Louis Youngblood. It appears that the negroes Tom, Louis and Charley Youngblood and another, a fugitive from justice in St. Helena parish, had been to a store where they had indulged freely in liquor. On their way home they passed a colored man who was feeding oxen with sweet potatoes, Louis asked for and received three pieces of sweet potato, one of which he offered Tom. This put him into a terrible rage and he commenced cursing Louis and attempted to cut his throat, Louis ran home followed by Tom; but Louis again made his escape and went to the house of another disreputable negro Peter Clark, his brother-in-law...

Thomas confronted his brother with a marble in a gun and shot his brother dead.[8]

The unspeakable tragedy of pain and chaos is part of the history of my Youngblood family. Thomas, only twenty-five years old and described as a light *griffe,* instead of being called mulatto, was now, in addition to being labeled a hoodlum, also labeled the murderer of his own brother. His fate is fixed in history to be read 136 years later. Is this story part of the whispered secrets among the descendants?

In March 1886, Governor Samuel D. McEnery of Louisiana issued and posted a proclamation in newspapers throughout the Florida Parishes for a $300 reward for the arrest of Thomas Youngblood.[9] I wanted and needed to see the original document that was at the Louisiana State Archives in Baton Rouge. And yes, I did see it.

The clerk placed a huge book on a table in front of me as genealogists Judy Riffel and Stephanie Martin Quiette looked on. Scrolling from one page to another it became obvious that it was standard practice to issue an Executive Order when a crime warranted an arrest.[10]

In addition to seeing the original Executive Order, I also found a newspaper article in *The Donaldsonville Chief* of Donaldsonville, Louisiana, dated 03 April 1886. This article showed that they were still searching for Thomas Youngblood as of that date. The headlines read,

---

[8] "Murder in Livingston Parish," *Maurepas (LA) Gazette,* Reported in the *Daily Advocate* (Baton Rouge, LA), March 18, 1884, p.4.

[9] "$300.00 Reward," *Daily Advocate* (Baton Rouge, LA), April 20, 1886, p.4.

[10] Executive Department – State of Louisiana for the arrest of Thomas Youngblood for killing his brother Louis Youngblood.

"Supposed Murderer Arrested."[11] The individual arrested was Monroe Youngblood, the brother of Thomas Youngblood.

> Robert Maple, the vigilant Constable of the sixth ward arrested on Monday last on the Clark Plantation, a colored man supposed to be Thomas Youngblood, who Killed his brother, Louis Youngblood, in the parish of Livingston some time during the month of June, 1883. The prisoner answers the description given in the Governor's proclamation offering $300 reward for his arrest and conviction, being black Negro, about 27 years of age, 5 feet 8 inches in height, weighs 165 pounds, has a broad face and uses a loud tone of voice when talking. He acknowledges that he is a brother of the murderer, but claims his name is Monroe Youngblood and not Thomas. Constable Maple landed his man in the parish jail, and the Sheriff of Livingston was promptly notified of the arrest by telegram. The arrival of an officer from that parish who can identify the prisoner is looked for daily.[12]

Wow! I wasn't expecting to turn over that stone. But I did find evidence listing Peter Clark as the brother-in-law of a Youngblood. The Youngblood connection is real. Now, I needed to see my twice-great-grandmother's name Rebecca in a census with Peter Clark.

---

[11] "Supposed Murderer Arrested." *The Donaldsonville (LA) Chief*, April 3, 1886, p.3.

[12] "Not the Man," *Donaldsonville (LA) Chief*, April 10, 1886, v. 15, p.4

Chapter 9
Finding Peter Clark

Peter Clark was enumerated twice as living in Ward 3 of St. Helena Parish and transcribed online incorrectly as *Peter Clorke*.[13,14] In one of the 1880 US Census records he was twenty-three years old and a laborer. He did not own property. His wife was Rebecca Clark, age eighteen, and she was also a laborer. They had two children—five-year-old Jane Clark and two-year-old Isabella Clark. Although the relationship was not described on this census, others in the household included forty-five-year-old Katie Bird (keeping house), and twenty-one-year-old Robert Clark, a laborer. All members of the household were born in Louisiana, including their mother and father.

The second search for Peter Clark was found on the microfilm in the 3rd Ward, page 17, supervisor 1, enumeration district 153, and this record is marked received on 16 August 1880. Peter Clark was twenty-eight years old and listed as a "Laborough" (laborer). He was born in

---

[13] Year: 1880; Census Place: 3rd Ward, St Helena, Louisiana; Roll: 468; Family History Film: 1254468; Page: 421A; Enumeration District: 153; Image: 0135.

[14] Year: 1880; Census Place: 3rd Ward, St Helena, Louisiana; Roll: 468; Page: 427A; Enumeration District: 153.

Louisiana, but according to *this* record, his mother and father were from Virginia. His wife Becky ("Peggy" transcribed online) was twenty-four and keeping house. She and both of her parents are from Louisiana. They had two children—six-year-old Harper listed as a son and one-year-old Isabella listed as daughter.[15] I cannot explain why in one census they showed two daughters and in another a daughter and a son. Perhaps, the census taker did not go to the house but relied on others in the neighborhood to provide that information.

The joy of finding that my grandmother's story about being named after her grandmother Rebecca was verified in the census record. Also, I saw my great-grandmother—Isabella Clark—as a toddler on both census records, and I remember her. She was born somewhere between 1879 and 1880.

I had confirmed the oral history of my grandmother's name. I now began to reflect on my great-grandmother Isabella.

---

[15] Year: 1880; Census Place: 3rd Ward, St Helena, Louisiana; Roll: 468; Page: 421A; Enumeration District: 153.

Chapter 10
Who is Isabella Clark?

My great-grandmother Isabella Clark's life had several twists and turns. She married her first husband, Henry Ernest Watson, about 1895 in Livingston Parish. Henry Ernest Watson reportedly disappeared without a trace.

However, my grandmother (MaBecky) always said that her father's name was Ernest Watson. I only discovered his full name when I found a letter dated April 23, 1958 (see below) that my grandmother wrote to Livingston Parish seeking her original marriage record. She mentioned her parents' names as Henry Watson and Isabella Clark.

> I am desirous of obtaining a copy of my marriage license issued during the year 1913, around November. The name is:
>
> Rebecca Mitchell (daughter of Isabella Clark and Henry Watson) of Maurepas, LA to Calvin Mitchell.
>
> License was taken at Centerville, Louisiana when that city was the County Seat.

I will be glad to pay whatever charges may be due, and am very anxious to have a copy of this certificate, so please advise at once and I will send whatever money may be needed....

P.S. The marriage was performed by the Tiger Bluff Baptist Church. We have written them but have not received any reply and would much prefer a copy of the license if same can be obtained. It is very important that I get this information in order to verify my birth record.[16]

Isabella had her baby girl Rebecca (MaBecky) christened at the Tiger Bluff Baptist Church in Maurepas.

Isabella worked odd jobs, and at one point lived and worked as a servant for Hillery S. Glasscock, a farmer in Livingston Parish, with her second husband, Henry Skinner.[17] That marriage did not last long, and later she married a Mr. Harris.

I remember sitting on the floor in my mother's house in New Orleans. Scanning the bedroom now converted into a den, I looked at an old picture on the wall—it was Mama Isabella, my great-grandmother. I took note of that majestic old picture portraying a woman with a haunting, distant stare, sitting with her arms draped backward on a chair. She seemed to be staring in my direction. This photograph was taken around 1914 in Maurepas. My mother mentioned that her grandmother Mama Isabella posed for that picture during a difficult time in her life. She was sad because of the death of her son, Berlin Watson. That photograph revealed her sadness.

Upon the birth of my mother, Isabella's only granddaughter, her mission in life changed. She devoted herself to getting the best education possible for her granddaughter, my mother.

Isabella had a lot of influence over my mother and encouraged my

---

[16] The original letter is in the Bernice Bennett Collection.

[17] Year: 1910; Census Place: Police Jury Ward 10, Livingston, Louisiana; Roll: T624_518; Page: 4A; Enumeration District: 0072; FHL microfilm: 1374531.

grandparents, Rebecca and Calvin Mitchell, to allow her to move to Madisonville in St. Tammany Parish. There she would attend a small private church school.

According to my Mother, her grandmother—Mama Isabella—did not want her to work in the fields. She knew that a better life and opportunities existed outside of Livingston Parish. After spending a brief time in St. Tammany Parish, Mama Isabella later followed her younger sister Hester Clark Robinson to New Orleans. They settled into Gert Town to live on Fern and Audubon Streets until her death in 1955.

Mama Isabella Harris with her Sunday School Class, 1947.
Bernice Bennett Collection.

The move to New Orleans put Mama closer to her cousins, Minerva, Josephine, Augustine, and Pinkie. These cousins were more like her sisters than her cousins. They had a close family bond that would continue throughout their lives and into death as some of them purchased cemetery plots near each other.

My Mama said that Mama Isabella and Isabella's sister, Aunt Hester, were always taking classes at night school. Isabella became a Sunday school teacher at the Greater King Solomon Baptist Church in New Orleans, and the members of her church called her "Sista Isabella."

As a little girl, my older sister Betty told me that she once called our great-grandmother "Sista Isabella." She received a scolding and the reminder that Mama Isabella was not her "Sista Isabella, but her great-grandmother Isabella."

A photo of Isabella in 1947 shows her standing among her young students on the steps of Greater King Solomon Baptist Church. Sitting on the first steps are my older siblings, Philip and Betty.

Upon my great-grandmother Isabella's death, her sister Hester Clark Robinson Quinn left a handwritten obituary:

On February 25, 1955

The Sweet Spirit of our dear mother and sister went to join the saviors in that home not built with hands but whose makers and builders is God. The daughter of Peter and Rebecca Clark, she was married to Ernest Watson and to this union two children was born Berlin Watson and Rebecca Watson. Berlin has passed to the great beyond. She became a Christian when quite young and was converted and joined the church and was baptized by Reverend E. Davis at Maurepas, Louisiana. She was always willing to do whatever she could to help in the master's cause. She moved to this city and was married to Mr. M. Harris who has passed to the great beyond. She joined Greater King Solomon church in 1936. She worked cheerful and faithful to the end. She leaves to mourn her lost [sic] one daughter Rebecca Mitchell, three grandchildren Bernice Alexander, Calvin and Spencer Mitchell, 2 sisters, Hester Quinn, Martha Reynolds and seven great grandchildren and a host of nieces, nephews and friends.

Life race well run, life work well done, and now she has gone home to live with God.

Isabella Clark Watson Skinner Harris (1879–1955).
Bernice Bennett Collection.

Chapter 11
Journeying Back in Time

Traveling back and forth to Livingston and St. Helena Parishes became part of my normal trips home to New Orleans. On one of those trips, I connected for the first time with Louisiana researcher Antoinette Harrell. She was welcoming and ready to share any information that could further my research on Peter Clark.

Antoinette Harrell is well known for her peonage research and advocacy work in Louisiana and the Mississippi Delta. She had her own public television show called *Nurturing Our Roots* that she broadcast out of New Orleans, and also a Blogtalkradio radio show. Her colleague and photographer/videographer Walter Black accompanied us to St. Helena Parish to capture the journey as Antoinette educated me on how to find the records I needed.

I took the same route from New Orleans to Greensburg, where the St. Helena Parish courthouse is located. This time, I saw large trucks hauling lumber up and down the highway. Clearly, timber was the major economic base in this area.

However, as I drove, I wondered how did the family live in St. Helena and Livingston Parish when they were not geographically close to each other. I asked folks in the St. Helena Courthouse about records in Maurepas, and they did not know what I was talking about. Then I remembered that Livingston Parish was not formed until around 1836. Portions of Ascension and St. Helena Parishes were divided to create Livingston Parish.

As I parked, I saw a white building that was the old land office adjacent to the courthouse, and the old jailhouse across the street. Of course, it was not used to house criminals anymore and served as a historical site. The vintage St. Helena Parish courthouse had that old moldy smell and was in need of a facelift. But it did have original records.

This visit was an eye-opener. In a small room of the courthouse I saw large books with indexes to deeds, wills, marriages. And other documents were stacked in rows or lined up on a table. But this was not the only thing waiting. A vault—yes, a vault—containing old metal file cabinets of all sizes. They filled the vault from the floor to the ceiling with documents dating back to the early 1800s. I had never seen anything like this in my life.

Antoinette asked me, "Bernice have you ever seen a crop lien?"

She opened a small metal container, pulled out a fragile and faded record, and with disgust told me that people lost their land by signing it over for money just to eat. They put liens on their property for as little as $25.00. We found wills and deeds and a document from a white Youngblood family meeting. They were discussing using their slaves as collateral to build a jail. This was most likely the jail that I saw when I parked my car earlier.

No sooner had I finished reading about the jail, when I spotted a metal file container with the marriage records.

I found them—Peter Clark and Rebecca Youngblood's marriage bond. I also discovered a copy of Rebecca's parents' marriage bond— Thomas Youngblood to Minerva Smith—as well the marriage bond of Peter's sister, Olivier Clark, to Alexander Dorsey, and the marriage record of Peter's brother, Bob Clark, to Emily Harrell. I was overwhelmed. My ancestors had touched those old fragile papers. I felt them standing behind me as my fingers felt the texture of the paper, and outlined the stroke of the X used as their signature. I closed my eyes to take in the moment and said a silent prayer, "Thank you, Lord!"

According to these records, a five-hundred-dollar matrimonial bond was issued in the State of Louisiana, Parish of St. Helena's Sixth Judicial District Court, for Thomas Youngblood to marry Minerva Smith on 17 August 1872. The witness to the bond was William H. Tillery, an attorney. Peter Clark and Rebecca Youngblood's five-hundred-dollar Matrimonial Bond was issued on 15 July 1874. Their matrimonial bond included the following information:

Be it Remembered that [sic] on this day of July 1874 that I the undersigned authority celebrated the rites of witness on between Peter Clark and Miss Rebecca Youngblood in the Presences of Gabsel Harris [sic] and Warner Doughty—competent witness all of the Parish of St. Helena State of Louisiana.

Gab Harris   Peter X (his mark) Clark
Warner X Doughty   Rebecca X (her mark) Youngblood

Subscribed to before me
This the 15th July 1874   W Woodmash [sic]
T.P. Ward

Well, look at this! Warner Doughty is a witness for Peter Clark. I had already seen the Doughty surname in the 1880 US census of families living near Peter and Rebecca. I noticed that my grandmother's first cousin—Cousin Minerva Robinson—also had bragging rights because she most likely was named after her great-grandmother Minerva Youngblood.

Overjoyed and overwhelmed, I slowly unfolded each document from that small metal cabinet. I could feel my ancestor standing next to me and was grateful to see records that they had touched and where they had signed their X.

I thought for a moment, *I wish that I could extract some DNA from those documents.* Just a thought because I knew it was impossible. However, I do carry the DNA of both Peter and Rebecca in me, so that is good enough for me.

Obtaining the marriage records gave me an even bigger incentive to keep moving backward and forward in my journey to find Peter Clark's land. Yes, I do mean backward and forward because I discovered that my plan sometimes was not linear, such as when I found the newspaper article on my twice-great-uncles. I did not expect it, but it became part of my story that verified the connection between Peter Clark and the Youngbloods.

One thing that I did not find in St. Helena Parish was any information on Peter Clark's land.

I returned to New Orleans on an emotional high and felt that my ancestors guided every step taken and every road traveled. Hence, I became determined that I would find Peter's land.

But before finding Peter's property, I wanted to know more about Thomas and Minerva Youngblood. Just imagine, I was looking for Peter Clark and Rebecca Youngblood and discovered my 3x-great-grandparents.

Chapter 12
The Farmer—Thomas Youngblood

In 1870, Thomas (43 years old) and Minerva Youngblood (35) were living in Ward 3 of St. Helena Parish with seven children— Thomas (10), Rebecca (12), Lewis (9), Charles (8), Marshall (6), Dave (5), and William (1).[18] Monroe Youngblood, the head of the household's brother mentioned earlier, was already old enough to be living in his own home.

Thomas Youngblood was the only Black farmer of the five individuals listed as farmers living near him on the census.

By 1880, Thomas Youngblood lived in Livingston Parish Ward 5, and my 3x-great-grandmother Minerva had passed away. He is still listed as a farmer, and the family has expanded.[19]

Louis (18) is still in the household with his siblings, Charles (16), Marshall (14), Henry (12), William (10), Roda Ann (8), and Pink (4).

Now, I was always on the hunt for Peter Clark's land but never expected to discover that my 3x-great-grandfather also owned property.

[18] Year: 1870; Census Place: Ward 3, St Helena, Louisiana; Roll: M593_529; Page: 97A; Family History Library Film: 552028.

[19] Year: 1880; Census Place: Livingston, Louisiana; Roll: 456; Page: 170A; Enumeration District: 138.

However, I could not find any documents to tell me how he acquired this land. I searched through old historical land records[20] and called the land office in Baton Rouge searching for any information on Thomas Youngblood's land.

The records in the Livingston Parish Courthouse were organized better than the St. Helena Parish Courthouse records. The research space was larger, and the big ledger books were spread out and organized for easy retrieval. The records room also had computers that would allow you to research by name and location. Hence, I took a chance and typed in Thomas Youngblood's name. Yes, they had a file on Thomas Youngblood.

> Parish of Livingston—State of Louisiana
> Succession [probate] of Thomas Youngblood
> Opposition to the Appointment of Robert Benefield
> Administrator
> Box 11
> File December 4th, 1882
> B Spiller—Clerk of Court

I could not believe what I was reading! Therefore I read each word—sometimes repeating them out loud.

> The opposition of the heir of Thomas Youngblood by Lewis Youngblood filed to the opposition of Robert W. Benefield for Administration on the succession of Thomas Youngblood deceased was taken pursuant to agreement and the law and the evidence being in favor of opponent and against the plaintiff applicant. It is broadly adjudged and decreed that the opposition be sustained and plaintiff application for administration said succession be rejected at the cost as in care of suit and

---

[20] I searched online for old historical land records in the Louisiana Division of Administration, Office of State Lands. https://wwwslodms.doa.la.gov/

plaintiff all cost incurred said application said opposition.

April 10, 1883
Jas M. Thompson
Judge 18th
District of Louisiana

Amazing! My twice-great uncles—the brothers of Rebecca Youngblood Clark—hired a lawyer to fight for their rights to handle their father's estate. The document read as follows:

ॐ

Succession of Thomas Youngblood
Note of Testimony
Filed May 8, 1883
Louis Harris, Clerk of Court

To the Hon James W. Thompson Judge of the Eighteenth District Court of the State of Louisiana—holdings [sic] of the same in and for the Parish of Livingston said State…

The petition of Lewis Youngblood as resident of said parish and the State respectfully represents That petitioner is the son of Thomas Youngblood deceased and over twenty one years old

That said succession of the petitioners father owns no debt

That Thomas Youngblood died two years ago or About

That his wife petitioners mother Minerva Youngblood died five years ago

That Robert Benefield has filed application to be appointed administrator of the succession of Thomas Youngblood deceased. That said Robert Benefield is not a creditor nor heir of said succession but an intermedler having no right to administer on the same there being no debts....

That petitioner is entitled to the administration of one succession.

Therefore petitioner prays that said Robert Benefield's application for the administration of the succession of Thomas Youngblood deceased be disallowed an[d] rejected at his cost and that said Robert Benefield pay all cost incurred in said succession and for general relief in the premises.

By WT Carter
Atty for the petitioner

Testimony of Robert Benefield

[sic] Robert Benefield being sworn says that he knows there was such a person as Thos Youngblood who died leaving a small estate knows there are minor heirs to that Estate—knows that the Estate owns debts.

Witness has a bill against the estate.

Mr. Watterson Notary Public refused to make an inventory of the said Estate.

Witness does not know that bill is correct don't know what the bill was for.

Defense offers Thomas Youngblood—who says he is the son of the deceased.

I no of no debts against the Estate—I paid all against the Estate—Mr. Wm Hammond never mentioned any claim to me he had against deceased—witness got Steve Ernest to pay the debts of decease—since debt of deceased witness has met Mr. Wm Hammond frequently and he never mentioned having any claim against the deceased.

Witness was over 22 years of age when his father died— says he knows that Wm Hammond knew that he, witness, was paying debts of the succession.

Wm Hammond asked me what I was going to do with the things of deceased and I told him I was going to pay his debts and carry on our business the same as deceased did. After this Wm Hammond hired me to work his effects and said nothing about any debts being due when he hired me.

Lewis Youngblood being sworn deposes that he is the son of the deceased and is 21 years old. His brothers paid all his father's debts he inquired for other debts and could find none. Mr. Hammond knew that father's debts were his paid and presented no account.

S. Ernest swore an[d] deposes—
I knew the deceased and his heirs—The heirs came to me—letter [illegible] and paid all the deceased owed us. Almost everyone knew that they were paying the debts. It was a public thing.

I saw one of the heirs working afterward for Hammond. There was posted notice of the payment of debts.

Rebutting

Benefield recalled. No evidence

This testimony had my head spinning. The brothers who were in unity supporting the opposition of the succession of their father's estate in May 1883 showed up a year later in 1884[21]; one was labeled as a hoodlum and murderer. The other was dead. And the article about the murder appeared in the *Maurepas Gazette*, owned and edited by Robert Benefield.

What was going on? In silence, I pondered whether to pursue any additional research concerning this matter or to just stay the course. I decided to just leave this mystery and continue to see what else I could discover on Peter Clark.

---

[21] "Murder in Livingston Parish," *Maurepas (LA) Gazette*, Reported in the *Daily Advocate* (Baton Rouge, LA), March 18, 1884, p.4.

Chapter 13
Freedom Has Arrived

So far most of my research focused on 1870 and forward. Now was the time for me to explore how far back I might find Peter Clark. Creating a timeline for Peter again was essential to finding his land. I wanted to walk down that road with him in his journey and his family.

Since I lived near the National Archives, I offered to help my friend Louisiana genealogist Leonard Smith locate his ancestors' records that might be in the Records of the Bureau of Refugees, Freedmen, and Abandoned Lands—better known as the Freedmen's Bureau—designated Record Group 105 in the National Archives.

I had all day to spend in the microfilm room, and had my coffee-stained handy reference pamphlet describing M1905—the book about the Freedman Bureau records. I knew exactly which microfilm reel—number 46—that might have the information I was seeking. The reel included Lafayette, Lafourche, Livingston, Morehouse, Natchitoches, Orleans, Ouachita, Plaquemines, and Pointe Coupee Parishes in Louisiana.

The microfilm room was dark and quiet. The only sound was the *swoosh* of the film moving through the microfilm feeder. As a teaser, I just scrolled through some of the records on the reel to orient myself to what I might find. I sat for a while and then stood up as if this would put me closer to the screen.

I finally reached Lafourche Parish on the reel and found the labor contract for Leonard's family. They were on the Rienzi Plantation owned by sugar planter Richard Allen. I was rejoicing that I found this record for Leonard when...*wait a minute!*

Yes, the next image was a labor contract in 1868 on the Coxe Plantation of Livingston Parish. At that time, that plantation did not mean anything to me. However, I had already decided to copy the entire reel of records for Livingston Parish anyway, and then I saw the next page.

I found the names Katie Clark (50), Ann Clark (18), Olivier Clark (16), Hester Clark (10), Peter Clark (9), Bob Clark (8), and Emma.

Katie Clark was listed as the mother of these children, and she is my 3x-great-grandmother. When I started the search I did not know if I would ever find Peter Clark's mother's name, or for that matter, his siblings. And now I was looking at a labor contract in Livingston Parish dated 7 April 1868, with the names of my family members.

As I read the terms of agreement, I had to comprehend what I was reading. I had this uneasy feeling that the freedmen and women were signing up to go back into slavery. The work hours and small wages did not seem a lot to me. However, I understood that the Freedmen for the first time would receive compensation to do what they had done when they were in bondage.

The regulation of written labor agreements between planters and freedmen was a major concern of the Freedmen's Bureau. In Circular Number 29 issued on December 4, 1865, Bureau officials in Louisiana outlined the rules governing the free labor system in the state. Freedmen could choose their employers, and all contracts were to be approved by a Bureau agent. Wages were not set, but the circular declared that it was the freedmen's "duty" to "obtain the best terms they can for their labor."

Freedmen were required to work twenty-six days per month, consisting of ten-hour days in the summer and nine-hour days in the winter. Any work time exceeding six hours beyond the normal workday would constitute an additional day's work. In addition to wages, freedmen were also entitled to receive rations, clothing, "comfortable" living quarters, and medical attention, and each family was to receive a half-acre plot to maintain a garden. Five percent of the freedman's monthly wages were to be retained by the employer for the purpose of sustaining schools for the freedman's children. In cases where freedmen desired to work for a share of the crop, employers were required to have sufficient amounts of provisions available for freedmen and their families each month. Also, employers who entered into share agreements were obligated to pay Bureau agents 1/20th of the amount of the freedmen's share of the crop each month for the benefit of freedmen schools.[22]

I read each word of the labor contract two, or maybe three times, and after seeing the words, I took a deep breath.

Katie Clark and her family have this day contracted and agrees: KATIE CLARK AND HER FAMILY...

Through teary eyes, with tissues in my hand, and now standing instead of sitting, I continued to read:

...He further agrees to pay unto Katie Clark and her family the sum of ($100) dollars for their work for this year and we the undersigned obligating themselves to work faithfully, and the at the legal number of hours each day. For misuse and neglect of the plowing stock and tolls we hold ourselves accountable. The party of the first part obligates himself to furnish free of charges boarding and lodging to undersigned. FMC

The signatures on the Coxe Plantation labor contract are Benjamin F. Coxe, William P. Coxe, Jon B. Easterly, and R.C. Webb.

---

[22] General Orders No.34, Plantation Regulations, Headquarters – Department of Mississippi, Vicksburg, Mississippi, March 23, 1865 – Major General N. J. T. Dana.

Chapter 14
Rethinking Peter's Surname

Armed with the names on the Freedmen's Bureau record, I thought that Peter had to be somewhere in Louisiana in the 1870 US Census. Why not search for Peter and his siblings by their first names rather than the last name and see what I could find?

I found him. He was right there in the 3rd Ward in St. Helena.[23] The surname was Johnson and not Clark. I don't know why the surname was Johnson other than seeing that other Johnsons are also living near Peter and his family.

I wondered who the Mary Johnson was in the household with Peter, because Peter's mother's name on the labor contract is Katie Clark. Could Mary be Katie? Was Katie's real name Mary Katherine? My head was spinning, and I had a feeling of doubt that this might not be my Peter.

But Olivier (listed online as Oliver) isn't just a coincidence when grouped with Hester and Bob. Ann and Emma are missing from this census and could be living in their own households. Bob was

---

[23] Year: 1870; Census Place: Ward 3, St Helena, Louisiana; Roll: M593_529; Page: 96B; Family History Library Film: 552028 – Peter is listed as Peter Johnson in the 1870 census.

consistently on all documents and also living with Peter in 1880. Plus they are in the same location in the 1880 US census. I decided to follow my gut! I believed in my heart of hearts that this was Peter and his family.

I shared those names with my mother, and she said, "Oh, your Aunt Hester was named after her Aunt Hester." Peter's sister. She then added a comment that just blew me away. She said that she knew Aunt Emma. The family lived with Aunt Emma and Uncle John Mack in New Orleans. *Wow! Double wow!* Mama was always throwing me nuggets of information, and I scribbled this comment on a pad with a note. *Find Emma.*

Taking a closer look at the 1870 US Census, I also noticed that William H. Tillery and Thomas Youngblood are also living near Peter Johnson. Oh yes, this was my Peter. Though I may never figure why so many Johnsons are listed in this particular census in the 3rd Ward of St. Helena Parish.

Chapter 15
Is Peter Clark a Homesteader?

Is it feasible to believe that Peter Clark obtained his land through the Homestead Act of 1862?

I have now traced Peter back as far as I wanted to go to get an idea of his location, and whether he owned land prior to 1900 as noted on that census.

His timeline was clear to me. He did not own any property between 1868 and 1880. During this time period, Peter Clark married Rebecca Youngblood, he had two children, and he put up a $500 marriage bond in 1881 for his brother Bob Clark to marry Emily Harrell, their next-door neighbor. I wondered if he voted?

Armed bodies of gangs known as the "buckshots," "the coal oil clan," or "the regulators" were known to kill people and burn houses to intimidate folks and keep them from voting. I'll never know if Peter voted or not because the Livingston Parish Courthouse burned down on

October 15, 1875. I could find no voter registration information on Peter.

I had so many thoughts as I reflected on Peter's life. I was humming one of Sam Cook's songs, "Change Is Gonna Come," and could not get that tune or the lyrics out of my head.

The fact is that Peter was born during a time when slavery was legal. However, as a child he may never have thought of himself other than as a free person because change was happening right before his eyes. I feel that the grapevine was alive and well when President Abraham Lincoln signed the Emancipation Proclamation granting some in Louisiana their freedom. And when the Civil War had officially ended, I suspect that rumors about the "forty acres and a mule" slated for Edisto Island may have also created tensions in the Louisiana parishes. I don't know where Katie and her children were before 1868. However, I feel that Katie did what she had to do when she agreed to the terms set forth on that Freedmen's Bureau labor contract.

Peter was an eyewitness to the political changes in Louisiana. He saw "over 133 Negro Legislators, of whom 38 were senators and 95 representatives." Three Negroes, Oscar J. Dunn, P.B.S. Pinchback, and C.C. Antoine, served as lieutenant governors. Pinchback was acting governor for forty-three days in the winter of 1873, when Henry C. Warmoth was removed from office. John W. Menard was elected to Congress, but was denied a seat. This occurred between 1868 and 1896.

I was then fixated on finding Peter's land. Did he buy this land? Was it a gift, or did Peter apply for a Homestead Patent under the Homestead Act of 1862?

I learned about this act through a class I had taken in 2009 with the National Institute of Genealogical Research (Gen Fed).

The federal Homestead Act of 1862 provided for the transfer of 160 acres of unoccupied public land to each homesteader on payment of a nominal fee after five years of residence. The government had previously sold land to settlers in the West. As the West became politically stronger, pressure was increased upon Congress to guarantee free land to others.

Was it possible to think that Peter Clark could be a Homesteader? After all, I don't ever recall seeing anything on TV or reading about Black Homesteaders. The one TV show I recall about homesteading is *Little House on the Prairie*, and they were white settlers.

I wondered if the Homestead Act of 1862 was intended to allow African Americans to own land because race designation is not included on any of the Homestead Applications. Yet the earlier homesteaders I read about were all white. Nevertheless, in 1872 the Homestead Act was extensively updated in section 2302 of the Revised Statutes of the Homestead Act, where it became illegal to make a "distinction on account of race or color."[24]

Yes, Peter Clark was a Homesteader. I obtained the application number 9590, and a certified copy of the original Homestead Certificate number 5887 issued on April 8, 1896, and signed by President Grover Cleveland from the Bureau of Land Management. Later, during a casual conversation, one of my cousins mentioned that she had the original copy of Peter's Homestead Certificate. She found it in an old book after one of Peter Clark's daughters, Hester Clark Robinson Quinn, passed away in 1986.

With the application number, I could order a copy of the original Homestead file for Peter Clark from the National Archives in Washington, DC.

Peter Clark applied for 159.33 acres of land on April 25, 1884, at the land office in New Orleans, Louisiana. According to the guidelines of the 1862 Homestead Act, Peter Clark had to live on, cultivate, and improve the property for five years. In addition, he had to meet the criteria to obtain the land:

1. Being a citizen or have the intent to become a citizen
2. Being a head of household, widow, or single male or female over the age of twenty-one
3. Not already owning 160 acres or more
4. Not having borne arms against the United States

---

[24] "Was Homesteading Only For White People?" (July 7, 2011) Friends of Homestead National Monument of America. [website]
http://homesteadcongress.blogspot.com/2011/07/was-homesteading-only-for-white-people.html

This was not an easy task because most applicants would need to have a small amount of money to apply for the land and then needed money to buy the farm tools to plow and cultivate the land. I doubt many people had those resources.

Oh, I was dancing and calling everybody who would listen to me to tell them about this discovery. But the prize was still waiting for me at the National Archives. I would see and touch the paper, smell the history, and look up toward the sky and rejoice that I had the original document to verify that my twice-great-grandfather Peter Clark owned a piece of land.

Waiting for the record felt like hours before it arrived on the second floor in the National Archives Research Room. I felt the stillness, heard no sound, and could just feel the intensity as each of the researchers opened boxes and large envelopes containing remnants of the past. I also felt like I was in a slow-motion movie, a very slow-motion movie indeed. Oh God, the waiting was killing me. Where was my record?

And then, I was handed a large grey box filled with papers folded in packets that included the Homestead Applications. I leafed through each envelope until I came to my packet. My beating heart was loud in this stillness as I was unfolding each piece of paper that had not been touched by any of Peter's descendants in over 115 years. Inhaling and exhaling, I felt self-conscious, because in this moment I could feel MaBecky, my grandmother; Mama Isabella, my great-grandmother; and Peter Clark, my twice-great-grandfather, all standing behind me waiting for me to read that first piece of paper.

> Peter Clark of Livingston Parish, Louisiana—patent application number 9590—Revised Statues of the United States, do solemnly swear that I am a native citizen of the United States over the age of 21 and head of a family.[25]

---

[25] Statement from Peter Clark of Livingston Parish, Louisiana—patent application number 9590, Homestead Certificate No. 5887.

The application included statements from two of four witnesses selected by Peter to verify that he lived and cultivated the land; receipts documenting application fees he paid; descriptions of the improvements Peter made to the land; newspaper notices announcing his intent to make final proof in support of his claim for the land; and a compelling description of how Peter almost lost his claim because he missed the final filing date in 1887.

After residing on the land for ten years, Peter was granted the land patent in 1896 for 159.33 acres of land located on the South East quarter of the North West quarter, the East half of the South West Quarter and the North West Quarter of the quarter of Section two, in the Township nine of the Range five East, South Eastern District East of the River of St. Helena Meridian in the Louisiana. See Appendix A for the full application.

Homestead Proof—Testimony of Claimant

Peter Clark, being called as a witness his own behalf in support of homestead entry, No. 9590, for SE ¼ of NW ½, E ½ of SW ¼ and NW ¼ of SW ¼ of Sec. 2TP.9S.R.5E.

Ques.1—What is your name, age, name, and post office:
Ans.—Peter Clark—38 years—Maurepas, Louisiana
Ques.2—Are you native-born citizen of the United States, and if so, in what State or Territory were you born?
Ans.—I am born in Louisiana.
Ques.3—Are you the identical person who made homestead entry, No 9590, at the New Orleans Land office on the twenty-fifth of April 1887, and what is the true description of the land now claimed by?
Ans.—I am—SE ¼ of NW ½, E ½ of SW ¼ and NW ¼ of SW ¼ of Sec. 2TP.9S.R.5E. SE District East of the Miss. River.

Ques.4—When was your house built on the land and when did you establish actual residences therein? (Describe said house and other improvements which you have placed on the land, giving total value thereof.)

Ans.—My house was built and I established actual residence on the land over 10 years ago. Dwelling $50.00, Outhouse $5.00, 5 acres fenced and cleared $50.00 = $105.00.

Ques.5—Of whom does your family consist; and have you and your family resided continuously on the land since first establishing residence thereof? (If unmarried, state the fact.)

Ans.—Of my wife and four children—We have lived on there continuously since first establishing residence.

Ques.6—For what period or periods have you been absent from the homestead since making settlement, and for what purpose; and if temporarily absent, did your family reside upon and cultivate the land during such absence?

Ans.—Not absent

Ques.7—How much of land have you cultivated each season, and for how many seasons have you raised crops thereon?

Ans.—About 5 acres for 10 years

Ques.8—Is your present claim within the limits of an incorporated town or selected site of a city or town, or used in any way for trade or business?

Ans.—It is not

Ques.9—What is the character of the land? Is it timber, mountainous, prairie, grazing, or ordinary agriculture land? State its kind and quality, and is what purpose it is most valuable.

Ans.—Piney-woods land—most valuable for farming when cleared.

Ques.10—Are there any indications of coal, salines, or minerals of any kind on the land? (If so, describe what they are, and state whether the land is more valuable for agricultural them for mineral purposes.)

Ans.—None whatever

Ques.11—Have you ever made any other homestead entry? (If so, describe the same.)

Ans.—I have not

Ques.12—Have you sold, conveyed, or mortgaged any portion of the land; and if so, to whom and for what purpose?

Ans.—I have not

Ques.13—Have you personal property of any kind elsewhere than on this claim? (If so, describe the same, and state where the same is kept)

Ans.—I have not

Ques.14—Describe legal subdivisions, or by number, kind of entry, and office where made, any other entry or filing (not mineral), made by you since August 30, 1890.

Ans.—I have made no other entry.

(Signed plainly with full Christian name.)

    his
Peter X Clark
    Mark

Although Peter answered the above questions, he almost missed the final filing date because he had difficulty raising money to pay for his transportation to New Orleans and other expenses. He pleaded his case as documented in his land entry file as follows:

Before me the undersigned authority, personally came and appeared Peter Clark who being by me first duty sworn, deposes and says that he is the identical person who made Homestead Entry No. 9590 on April 25, 1887;

that the seven years in which homesteaders are required to make Proof in support of the entries expired in his case on April 25, 1894 and his final Proof made this day in support of his said Entry #9590 is not within the statutory period. That he is a very poor man and that until today he has not been able to get money to pay the cost of making proof and this is the earliest day he had the money.

That he has lived on and cultivated his land in good faith for over ten (10) years and it would work a great hardship, were he deprived of his entry. Wherefore, he prays that his Proof be accepted passed, his Final Certificate Receipt and issue thereon and that he may receive Patent on his said entry after the necessary formalities in the provisos—Sworn to and subscribed

his
Peter X Clark
Mark

Before me A.D., 1894 G. McD. Brumby—Register

After pleading his case, Peter Clark received his Homestead Land Patent in 1896.

Chapter 16
Follow the Witnesses—Am I My Brother's Keeper?

With excitement and pride I called my mother to tell her I had papers to verify that Peter Clark, her great-grandfather, owned land in Maurepas. My mother asked me to slow down after hearing me rattle off the names of the witnesses. She was processing what I had to say. So, as slowly as I could, I read each name to her—Henry Tinkshell, Charles Baptiste, Marshall Douglass, Alfred Robinson, Robert Benefield. It was my hope that those names might trigger recognition of someone in her past.

Without hesitation Mama said, "Yes, Charley Baptiste[26] is a close family friend to Mama Isabella—her grandmother. He had a brother named Pete, and two sisters, Delphine and Jane."

I remembered seeing Charley's name in that big old family Bible. His name was also listed as a witness to my grandmother MaBecky's wedding in 1913. That recognition alone set me in a new direction to follow each of those witnesses.

---

[26] Charlie, Charles, Charley had several spellings for his surname—Baptiste, Batice, and Batiste.

This discovery felt like a community of friends and family who had something to do with Peter Clark acquiring his land.

Suppose the witnesses for Peter Clark were also Homesteaders? Could they also be African Americans? And Robert Benefield, wait a minute, wasn't he the same man who tried to do the succession in 1883 on my 3x-great-grandfather Thomas Youngblood's land? And wasn't he the man that wrote a newspaper story about my twice-great-uncle's murder and called Peter Clark disreputable? Ok, I cannot tell this story without a little thought of a conspiracy theory. Especially since the Benefields and Peter Clark were neighbors in the 1900 census.

One more thing—Henry Tinkshell and Charlie Baptiste were living next to my 3x-great-grandfather Thomas Youngblood in the 1880 census and also on the agriculture census near him.

This was a bigger story. Mama wanted to know more and encouraged me to keep looking.

I imagined this scenario: These men met in a cabin near Lake Maurepas and decided that they would help each other acquire land by serving as witnesses for each other. They each applied for the land. When it was time to testify, they kept their promises and signed on the dotted line. This signature meant that the homesteader had complied with the guidelines to acquire the land. So, can I make this fantasy or theory come true?

I had a research plan to confirm or deny my theory. This included searching for online verification through the Bureau of Land Management. I wanted to determine if any of the witnesses to Peter Clark's were Homesteaders. If they were Homesteaders, I could order their files from the National Archives. If they were not listed as Homesteaders, I would search the Freedman's Bank and Trust Records and also look for voter registration information. If this search did not yield any information, I would then look for Civil War Pension Records.

I found myself on a research journey to find the story. I needed to know how these men interacted in the community and their relationship to Peter Clark.

I confirmed one theory with ease through the Bureau of Land

Management and four of the witnesses were also Homesteaders.

Charles Baptiste
Application Number 9844
Homestead Certificate Number 5274

Alfred Robinson
Application Number 15940
Homestead Certificate Number 8102

Henry Tinkshell
Application Number 8854
Homestead Certificate Number 5376

Robert K. W. Benefield
Application Number 9621
Homestead Certificate Number 2062

Chapter 17
Guided by Faith and Fantasy

I discovered that one of the witnesses, Marshall Douglass, was not a Homesteader but a member of Company D, 4th Volunteer Regiment of United States Colored Calvary. Marshall applied for a Civil War Invalid Pension Record.[27] My mother told me several stories about the Civil War. I believe that those stories came from her grandmother Isabella, who may have known Marshall Douglass, a friend of her father, Peter Clark.

Marshall Douglass entered the Civil War at the age of eighteen years by draft on 1 September 1864, and was discharged on 20 March 1866. He was born in St. Landry Parish and was a laborer. Formerly enslaved, his slave owner was not named on his pension application.

Marshall's marriage in 1878, performed by Reverend Charles Brooks, ended in divorce in 1892. His two children were Augusters Douglass born on 24 April 1888, and Noretta Douglass born on 7 March 1891.

Testifying on his behalf, B.W. Benefield, a citizen of Maurepas,

---

[27] Soldier's Application for Pension—Under the Act of June 27, 1890 – Marshall Douglass – Company D, 4th Regiment, USC Calvary – Certificate Number 684014. NARA I.

stated in Marshall's pension application,

> I did not know the soldier previous to enlistment, have
> been acquainted with him about 15 years and have
> observed him closely, live about two miles from him, I
> find that he suffers from a wound caused by a horse
> falling on his hand at the Battle of Clinton, La. He can
> neither close nor open his hand.

As I continued to read the pension file, I stopped dead in my tracks when the names H.N. Tinkshell residing at Maurepas Parish of Livingston, and B. Frazier were listed as witnesses on behalf of Marshall Douglass. H.N. Tinkshell was also a witness for Peter Clark's Homestead Application. I discovered that Benjamin Frazier was a witness on my grandmother's 1913 wedding license. This is not a coincidence. I am feeling the community. But I needed to continue to make sense out of what I was uncovering.

This small rural community in Louisiana has a bigger story to tell about how family, friends, and neighbors helped each other.

My hunch about the potential Homesteaders has paid off, because the next witness I reviewed was Henry N. Tinkshell. Thirty-six-year-old Henry Tinkshell applied for his Homestead on 10 October 1885. I suspect that he was a friend of my 3x-great-grandfather Thomas Youngblood since they lived near each other in 1880.

Henry Tinkshell, the second witness for Peter Clark, stated that he built a house in 1880 and "cleaned up a little land for a garden valued at $25.00." He lived there all the time and even voted in the 5th precinct: "I voted there last and has voted there ever since."

He had a family consisting of his wife, Corrine, one child, his mother—Helen Brook—and his niece, Jane Penn. His house was about 25 feet x 26 feet, consisting of four rooms built out of cypress wood, a corn crib, a kitchen, and fences that were together worth $250. He also had one horse, seven head of cattle, and a few hogs.

Charles Baptiste was a witness for Henry Tinkshell. Charles was the same person who witnessed Peter Clark's application. But he was not the only witness. I also see F.F. Landry, E.L. Landry, and G.A. Vidal on the list as witnesses. Charles Baptiste was listed as mulatto on the 1880 US census.[28] He also lived near Henry Tinkshell and Thomas Youngblood, Peter Clark's father-in-law.

Edmund Landry, a witness for Henry Tinkshell, noted that Peter Baptiste and A. Vidal "live nearer to Henry than he did." My mother mentioned Pete Baptiste when I called her—he was Charles Baptiste's brother. A. Vidal is actually Gumersindo Adriene Vidal, a former officer in the United States Colored Troops.

Thirty-five-year-old Frederick F. Landry was a farmer and a lumberman. He had known Henry for about ten years and had seen Henry Tinkshell "pretty near every day."

Edmund Landry made it clear that he lived near Henry and had seen him with his family there: "I saw him there yesterday."

Every witness was telling a story about how they were acquainted with each other.

When it came to Robert Benefield, I had already looked up his profile in *Herringshaw's Encyclopedia of American Biography in the Nineteenth Century*, published in 1898. Robert Benefield was a journalist and planter, born December 28, 1835, in Louisville, Kentucky. He attended the Ayers University, of Albany, Ind., and was a graduate of the American Health College of Cincinnati, Ohio. He served as a private soldier in the Confederate army. He was the editor and owner of the *Southland and Gazette*, of Maurepas. He had been a justice of the peace, a member of the school board, and had held various other public offices in his county and state.[29]

Robert K.W. Benefield, the witness for Peter Clark, was also a Homesteader. Fifty-two-year-old Robert was listed as an editor and also a merchant on his Homestead application of 9 May 1887. He lived at

---

[28] Year: 1880; Census Place: Livingston, Louisiana; Roll: 456; Page: 170A; Enumeration District: 138.

[29] "Robert K. W. Benefield." *Herringshaw's Encyclopedia of American Biography of the Nineteenth Century.* Chicago, IL: American Publishers' Association, 1898, p.103.

Catfish Bluff in Livingston Parish and first settled there in 1871. About four acres of lumber had been cut and removed from the land before he settled there, and he had cleared another seventeen acres since.

Robert's first wife died in March 1879 on the homestead. Her death broke up his home, and he was compelled to live in Ponchatoula for several months during the years 1880 and 1881.[30] He remarried in 1881, and noted in his homestead application that his present wife and two children were in the house.

Robert's dwelling was a 20 feet x 24 feet box or plank house and worth about $400. Brunson, a carpenter, built this house in 1872. Benefield had a Printing Office with contents worth about $5,000. He also had a well, fencing, and an orchard and garden. The total value of the improvements was $1,500. He reported that he had a good horse that he lost in the previous year, two oxen, and nine head of cattle, three sheep, ten hogs, twelve chickens, two dogs, and one cat. In addition, he listed his furniture: two tables, six chairs, one bureau, two trunks, a library including books in his printing office. All this was valued at $2,000. He also had an organ and a sewing machine.

One of Robert Benefield's witnesses to his application, Sandford Webber, noted that Peter Clark and George L. Jones lived nearer to Robert then he did. This was in response to a question about the names of other individuals that live nearer to Benefield.[31]

Alfred Robinson, another witness, was Black and also a Homesteader. I was excited! It is an empowering experience to uncover the stories of African-American homesteaders in Maurepas. I had no idea that my theory would be confirmed.

Forty-four-year-old Alfred Robinson established his actual residence in 1894 and his homestead in 1893. His dwelling consisted of

---

[30] Year: 1880; Census Place: Ponchatoula, Tangipahoa, Louisiana; Roll: 471; Page: 527B; Enumeration District: 184.

[31] Sanford Webber – Homestead, Pre-Emption and Commutation Proof: Testimony of Witness – November 14, 1887. Homestead Entry Papers - Original Entry Number No: 9620 for Claimant – Robert K.W. Benefield – Land Office – New Orleans, Louisiana – Approved – Thomas Butler – Register.

a house, with a kitchen and outhouse valued at $250. He had a wife and seven children, and lived on about four acres for five years.

Alfred's witnesses were Valson Fortenot, Charles Perkins (this name is in the family Bible), John Smiley, and Henry Tinkshell. This is the third homestead application where Henry Tinkshell is serving as a witness. But wait! On 29 July 1899, Alfred Robinson had another list of witnesses that included John Smith, Henry Tinkshell, S. Rousseau, and Peter Clark. On this second list of witnesses Henry Tinkshell and Peter are the only African Americans.

The Register that approved Alfred Robinson's Homestead Land Application was Walter L. Cohen. Walter L. Cohen, Sr., was an African-American Republican politician and businessman in Louisiana.[32]

Charles Baptiste is the final witness for Peter Clark. He is in the family Bible, and as mentioned earlier, he witnessed my grandmother's marriage in 1913. Thirty-five-year-old Charles Baptiste of Maurepas, Louisiana, applied on 11 August 1887, for his Homestead. He is the only applicant I have read about where he stated that his house is on "his original farm and that was built 20 years earlier." This house consisted of two rooms, a kitchen, one well, and "about seven to eight acres fenced on his original and adjoining farm valued at $500. He was not married, and his mother was dependent on him for support. He had lived continuously on his farm for twenty years.

Charles named as his witnesses Ovide Alexis, M.F. Bradford, Mike Harris, and Adrien Vidal. Adrien Vidal is the same G.A. Vidal who served as a witness for Marshall Douglass's Civil War Invalid Pension.

Searching for more information about Charles, I discovered a Freedman's Bank and Trust record issued for his half-brother Joseph Colbert. At the age of thirty-one, Joseph Colbert served as a stevedore in New Orleans. He had a wife named Martha and a daughter, Annie. He did not know his father but indicated that his mother was Matilda

[32] "Leading the Way: Walter Louis Cohen." *The New Orleans Tribune.* (2017). [website] http://www.theneworleanstribune.com/main/leading-the-way-walter-louis-cohen/

Baptiste and his stepfather was John Baptiste. His brothers are Clovice, Pete, and Charley, and sisters are Jane, Lizzie, and Delphine. I felt confident that my mother clearly knew what she was speaking of when she named Charles Baptiste's siblings.

Charley Baptiste (or Batice) was the only Black Homesteader I identified who conveyed six acres of land at $150 in 1911 to the School Board of Livingston Parish for the purpose of public education.[33]

As I continued to review Homestead applications, I wondered how many times did these witnesses support each other in the application process?

Could the relationships go beyond the Homestead applications? Could I find other events in the community such as marriages, work life, and religious affiliations? This was a challenge because I needed to dig deeper into the community to track each Homesteader.

The connections astounded me. This was no longer a list of names and basic information. These are concrete relationships:

- Charles Baptiste's sister Jane Doughty's son Clovice Russell married Peter Clark's daughter Mary (Dollie) Clark.
- Charles Baptiste's sister Delphine married Gumersindo Adriene Vidal, and she was my grandmother's school teacher.
- Benjamin Frazier and Charles Baptiste were witnesses for my grandmother Rebecca Watson's marriage to Calvin Mitchell.
- Robert Benefield filed a petition to serve as the executor of my 3x-great-grandfather's Thomas Youngblood's estate when he died around 1882.
- Benjamin Frazier is also a former soldier in the United States Colored Troops and a Homesteader, and Marshall Douglass served

---

[33] Chas.Batice to School Board of Parish of Livingston – State of Louisiana filed and recorded November 3, 1911. Record 497 – 10854 A (Six acres of land more or less, described as follows, beginning at the step[sic] at intersection of Tiger Bluff Public road with the White Hall Public Road, running West said White-Hall Public road: 340 yards to a post; thence North 100 yards to branch; thence East along branch to a steb[sic] on Tiger Bluff Public; Thence South 100 Yards to starting point.

as a witness for him.

It took hours and hours of research to uncover these connections. I wish that my mother and grandmother were alive to see what I had discovered. Just finding African-American Homesteaders is a major finding because race is not mentioned in any Homestead application. This meant that I had to order the homestead land entry file, analyze it, and then look at the census to determine if they were Black or White.

As a descendant of Homesteader Peter Clark, I am proud that my ancestor chose to exercise his rights and freedom to acquire 159.33 acres of land. In fact, Blacks in this small rural village in Livingston Parish demonstrated their ability to complete the application process with the help of family and friends. White and Black men supported each other in spite of the political climate from Reconstruction to hideous Jim Crow laws and the terror of Klansman in this Parish. Even Henry Tinkshell dared to vote and made it clear in his Homestead Entry papers that he voted.

The political and racist climate did not make it easy for African Americans to vote. This came to light in sworn testimony at the hearings of the Commissioner of the United States Circuit Court in Louisiana regarding the 1876 Elections. Many Blacks were intimidated at the ballot box and also threatened, beaten, and even had their homes burned to the ground to prevent them from voting. Yet, they persisted at the ballot box and also with their applications to obtain the land. This is a part of the American promise of freedom.

These men did not pack their bags and migrate to Kansas[34] as many Black families did during the early nineteenth-century because they were fed up with the political factions in Louisiana that prevented them from making a living, and enjoying freedom as any other American. Peter Clark and his community of family and friends remained in Louisiana to fight the fight for the opportunity to own land.

---

[34] Painter, Nell Irvin. *Exodusters; Black Migration to Kansas After Reconstruction.* New York: W.W.Norton and Company, 1986.

Chapter 18
What Happened to Peter Clark's Land?

I realized that with all my questions answered about Peter Clark's land, I still felt a pull to find out what happened to his land. Mama was also curious. We took one more trip to the Livingston Parish Courthouse to find something, anything, to help us close this chapter in our research. Little did I know that this would be my mother's last journey with me because she died in 2010, ten months after we found our answer about the status of Peter Clark's property.

The trip began as all trips with Mama searching for another Butterfly pin and the same giddiness about her that always began with a forgotten memory.

Peter Clark's adult children had slowly moved off the land to create new homesteads for their families in Livingston, St. Landry, St. Tammany, and Orleans Parishes. We did not realize that the land was still part of Peter Clark's estate.

I even found a transaction in the courthouse where in 1903 Peter sold B.B. Cleaney a small piece of property for $25.00.

However, by 1918, nine years after Peter's death, I discovered an order to seize and sell Peter's property. The administrator of the property was Peter's son, William Clark.

Simpson H. Sharp, sheriff of Livingston Parish seized the property—One hundred fifty-nine and 33/100 acres (159.33) of the defendant, William Clark.[35]

The advertisement in the *Denham Springs News*, a weekly newspaper, was published for thirty days and noted that the property would be sold on the front door of the courthouse in the town of Centerville on Saturday, 26 October 1918.

Peter's son, William Clark (the plaintiff) and William B. Kemp (his lawyer) went to the courthouse door. After the property was appraised at about one o'clock, the first order of seizure for the sale was read. The mortgage certificate, the oath of the appraisers, and the appraisement of the property were posted at public auction, and everyone was invited to bid.

Clinton Stegall bid for William B. Kemp the price of one hundred and fifty dollars for the interest of William Clark. Then the last and highest bid was received for two-thirds of the appraisement in the interest of William Clark. William B. Kemp obtained the property for the price of one hundred and fifty dollars. This purchaser allowed William Clark to retain the property.

William Clark did retain the property for his own free use.

---

[35] William Clark to William B. Kemp: William B. Kemp vs. #1185 William Clark - 25th Judicial District Court, Parish of Livingston , Louisiana. #18852A – 413.

"Whereas, I Simpson M. Sharp. Sheriff of the above said Parish and State and virtue of an order to seize and sell issued out of the above Court, in the above numbered and entitled cause, and in compliance with said order, I seized the property of the defendant, William Clark, described as follows: All his undivided interest in and to the S. E. 1/4 of N.W. 1/4, E.1/2 of S.W. 1/4 and N.W. 1/4 of S.W. I/4 of Section Two (2), T. 9. S. R. 5. E., Southeastern District of Louisiana, in said Parish and State, containing One hundred and Fifty-nine and 33/100 acres (159.33).

"In Testimony whereof, I, have hereunto signed my name officially, at my office, in Centerville, said Parish and State, on this 26th October 1918. Truly Recorded in Sheriff's Sale Book "C" Pge. 124 & 125, October 26, 1918. Simpson M. Sharp - Sheriff of the Parish of Livingston, Louisiana. (U.S. Documentary Stamps in the sum of 50 cents affixed and same are duly cancelled). File for record October 28th, 1918. Louis R. Kimball—Clerk of Record."

However, other transactions were found to show that problems were still plaguing the descendants. With the failure to pay taxes, the family members moved to other parishes. It appears that the land was abandoned.

I later discovered a lawsuit filed in 1965, at the Livingston Parish Clerk of Court: *Barbara Dendinger Brown vs. the heirs of Peter Clark.*[36]

My determination to follow this land to the end brought me to a shocking document where Barbara Dendinger Brown, a business owner, sued the heirs of Peter Clark in 1965 for full rights to the property.

What follows is testimony describing what happened to the land. It was written in 1944 and was included in the 1965 legal case.

Steve Lauzervich and Royal Lauzervich of Maurepas were familiar with Peter Clark's property. The land was described as all wooded with about one-half being highland and the remainder in the tidewater swamp.

> That about 60 years ago Peter Clark, colored, was living on the tract with his family. Improvements consisted of a dwelling house and other farm buildings. About 30 acres of the tract was fenced and cultivated by Clark until his death about 45 years ago. Some of his family lived on the North portion of the land for several more years, the last persons moving off of the property about 40 years ago with all improvements disappearing through neglect. Since that time there have been no improvements on the land and none of it has been enclosed by fence.

> Simpson Sharp brought in the tract for taxes about thirty-five years ago and sold it to the Dendinger Company about twenty-five years ago. About fifteen or twenty

---

[36] Twenty-first Judicial District Court, parish of Livingston, State of Louisiana. No. 14,236-Division "A," Barbara Dendinger Brown vs. Heirs of Peter Clark, 11 June 1965. Reference, tax deeds record COB 39 and COB 40, p.314.

years ago, T. A. Tycer, Surveyor, surveyed the tract for the Dendinger Company. At that time the lines around the tract were well-marked with blazes, and these lines can still be located at the present time. This survey did not encroach on any of the adjoining property owners.

About 15 or 20 years ago the Dendinger Company cut timber over the entire tract, working on the land for several months. About 7 or 8 years ago the present owner, Barbara Dendinger Brown, had some pine timber cut on the highland portion of the land.

That to the best of the affiants' knowledge and belief the present owner of the caption land, Barbara Dendinger Brown and her predecessors is title, have enjoyed open and peaceable and continuous possession of the caption land for more than 50 years and we have never known of any adverse claims or any encroachment by adjoining property owners.

The lawyer who purported to represent the heirs of Peter Clark documented that he could not find any evidence that Peter owned the land in question. Others had been trying to get the land since Peter's death in 1909, and the failure to pay taxes and other factors may have led to the complete loss of the family land.

The Dendinger Company had a long history of owning sawmills in St. Tammany and Livingston Parishes. With the land in arrears for unpaid taxes, Dendinger Brown found a way to own and then claim the rights to the property by suing the heirs in 1965.

Crying and shaking my head, I read this testimony and all the other documents associated with the loss of my twice-great-grandfather's property. I just had a hard time accepting that my grandmother MaBecky, her Aunt Hester, and several hundred heirs who were all alive and residing in Livingston and Orleans Parishes even

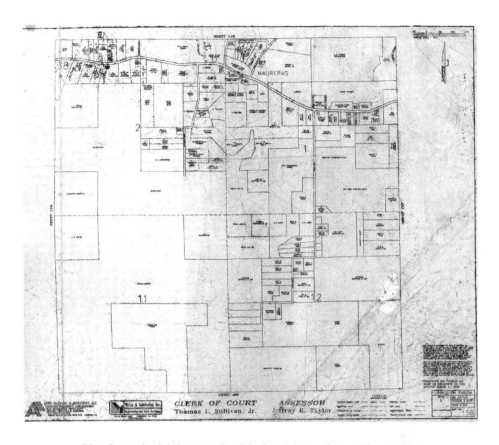

Plat from the Livingston Parish, Louisiana, Court House. The number 2 in the upper left quadrant of the plat is where Peter Clark's land was located. Bernice Bennett Collection.

knew about this lawsuit. My grandmother lived a long life, and always spoke of this land owned by our family. How could this have happened?

I wanted to follow the land to the end. When I provided the land coordinates to the Livingston Parish Clerk of Court, I was given a copy of the plat of the land once owned by Peter Clark. At the time I received the plat, I asked for the name of the present owners and was informed that the land was sold to Weyerhaeuser, the large paper and lumber company.

Reflections!

Just imagine, I kept my grandmother's story alive by remembering her simple words, "My granddaddy owned a lot of land in Maurepas, Louisiana." This clue set the stage for a wonderful journey back in time.

When I set out to verify her story, I never envisioned that this journey would lead me through several twist and turns of discovering a bigger story about my family and the community. I just wanted to find my twice-great-grandfather Peter Clark's land. However, the question of whether he owned land forced me to examine and weave together an array of documents and events to help me tell a bigger story about family, freedom, tragedy, community, and love.

My 15-plus year journey to find my twice-great-grandfather's land would never have taken place if I did not have the oral history of my grandmother MaBecky. The support from my dear Mother made this journey so powerful and endearing.

I did not know the names of my 3x-great-grandparents, Thomas Youngblood and Minerva Smith, until I knew oral history from my grandmother's story that she was named after her grandmother Rebecca Youngblood. Just searching for Rebecca brought me to her parents and siblings in St. Helena Parish. Even Rebecca's parents' 1872 marriage bond[37] was found at the courthouse as well as the marriage bond of Rebecca to Peter Clark, in 1874.

Also, because of DNA testing, I have verified and connected with the descendants of Peter Clark's sister Elizabeth Olivier Dorsey; his daughter Martha Clark, and his daughter Hester Clark Robinson Quinn.[38] I also connected with descendants of Thomas and Minerva Smith Youngblood via DNA. And the most amazing part of this journey was to connect with the Watson family and attend the Watson Family Reunion. I felt my grandmother smiling because DNA connected the missing links and made all this possible.

It is my hope that individuals in Livingston and St. Helena Parishes will also take up the task and find out how their ancestors owned a lot of land.

Each step in my journey lined up with the others, and some painful information was uncovered in this process. So painful that I never heard that story shared among the family members.

Oral history is a powerful tool, and I am grateful that I listened to my grandmother's story about her grandfather Peter Clark and was able to forever remember this journey of Searching for Granddaddy's Land in Livingston Parish.

---

[37] Matrimonial Bond – State of Louisiana—Parish of Helena: Sixth Judicial District Court.

"Thomas Youngblood as principal, and WH Tillery as security, held and firmly bound unto the Clerk of said court, and his assigns in the sum of five hundred dollars, to which payment, well and truly to be made, we bind ourselves, our heirs, and assigns, etc.

"Whereas, the above bond Thomas Youngblood has applied to said Clerk for a License to enter into the bonds of Matrimony with Minerva Smith 8-17-1871 – Filed September 17, 1871." (Original copy obtained from the St. Helena Courthouse in Greensburg, Louisiana in 2006.

[38] 23andme and Ancestry.com DNA companies.

Appendix A
Peter Clark's Homestead Land Entry Papers[39]

Application No 9590, Land Office at New Orleans,
Louisiana
April 25, 1887

I, Peter Clark, of Livingston Parish Tiger Bluff P.Sa, do
hereby apply to enter, under Section 2289, Revised
Statues of the United States, the SE1/4 of NW, E1/2 of
SW1/4 of Section 2, in Township of South Range 5
Home of the S.E.Dist of Miss River, containing one
hundred fifty nine 33/100 acres.

His
PETER X CLARK
Mark

---

[39] Peter Clark Land Entry Papers – Homestead Certificate No. 5887. Application #
9590. National Archives and Records Administration I.

4-772

The United States of America,

TO ALL TO WHOM THESE PRESENTS SHALL COME, GREETING:

Homestead Certificate No. 5887

Application 9590

Whereas there has been deposited in the GENERAL LAND OFFICE of the United States a CERTIFICATE of the Register of the Land Office at *New Orleans, Louisiana*, whereby it appears that, pursuant to the Act of Congress approved 20th May, 1862, "To secure Homesteads to actual settlers on the public domain," and the acts supplemental thereto, the claim of *Peter Clark* has been established and duly consummated in conformity to law for the *South East quarter of the North West quarter, the East half of the South West quarter and the North West quarter of the South West quarter of Section two in Township nine South of Range five East, South Eastern District East of River of St Helena Meridian in Louisiana, containing one hundred and fifty nine acres and thirty-three hundredths of an acre,*

according to the Official Plat of the Survey of the said Land returned to the GENERAL LAND OFFICE by the SURVEYOR GENERAL.

Now know ye, That there is therefore granted by the UNITED STATES unto the said *Peter Clark* the tract of Land above described, TO HAVE AND TO HOLD the said tract of Land, with the appurtenances thereof, unto the said *Peter Clark* and to his heirs and assigns forever.

In testimony whereof I, *Grover Cleveland* President of the United States of America, have caused these letters to be made Patent, and the Seal of the General Land Office to be hereunto affixed.

Given under my hand, at the City of Washington, the *eighth* day of *April*, in the year of Our Lord one thousand eight hundred and *ninety six*, and of the Independence of the United States the one hundred and *twentieth*.

By the President: *Grover Cleveland*

By *M. McKean* Secretary.

L. Q. C. Lamar Recorder of the General Land Office.

101

Appendix B
Land Office at New Orleans, Louisiana

April 25, 1887

I, Thomas J. Butler, REGISTER OF THE LAND OFFICE, do hereby certify that the above application is for Surveyed Lands of the class which the applicant is legally entitled to enter under Section 2289, Revised Statutes of the United States, and that there is no prior valid adverse right to the same.

Thomas J Butler
Register
(5760-40M).
(4_138)

Receiver Duplicate Receipt No. 9590   Application No. 9590

HOMESTEAD

Receiver's Office, New Orleans, La.
April 25th, 1887

RECEIVED of Peter Clark the sum Eighteen dollars No cents: being the amount of fee and compensation of Register and Receiver for the entry of SE 1/4 of NW 1/4, E 1/2 of SW 1/4 and NW 1/4 of SW 1/4 of Section of 2 in Township 9 South, of Range 5 East former SE Dist., under Section 2290, Revised Statutes of the United States

Receiver

$18.00

One hundred and fifty nine and 33/100 acres.

Note: It is required of the homestead settler that he shall reside upon and cultivate the land embraced in his homestead entry for a period of five years from the time of filing the affidavit, being also the date of entry. An abandonment of the land for more than six months works a forfeiture of the claim. Further, within two years from the expiration of the said five years he must show proof of his actual settlement and cultivation, failing to do so which, his entry will be canceled. If the settler does not wish to remain five years on his tract, he can, at any time after six months, pay for it with cash or land warrants, upon making proof of settlement and cultivation date of filing affidavit to the time of payment

❧

(4-063)

HOMESTEAD

(AFFIDAVIT)

LAND OFFICE at New Orleans, LA
April 25, 1887

I, Peter Clark, of Livingston Parish, La. Having filed my application, No. 9590, for an entry under Section No. 2289, Revised Statutes of the United States, do solemnly swear that I am a native citizen of the United States and over the age of twenty one years and the head of the family that said application, No.9590, is made for the purpose of actual settlement and cultivation; that said entry is made for my own exclusion benefit, and not directly or indirectly for the benefit or use of any other person or persons whomsoever; and that I have not heretofore had the benefit of the homestead laws.

Peter x Clark
Mark
Sworn to and subscribed this Twenty fifth day of April 1887, before Thomas J Butler
Land Office
Register

Note, If this affidavit be acknowledged before the Clerk of the Court, as provided for by Sec.2294, U.S. Revised Statues, the homestead part must expressly state herein that he or some member of his family is residing upon the land applied for, and that bona fide improvement and settlement have been made. He must also state why he is unable to appear at the Land Office.

ELECTRO'S (477—25,000)

[Writing included on the side of the application form:]

See note, which Clerks of the Courts and Registers and Receivers will read and Explain Thoroughly to persons making application for lands where the affidavit is made before either of them. (See directions to Land Officers on Duplicate Receipt.)

ॐ

(4—348.)

No. 1—HOMESTEAD.
Land Office at New Orleans, La.
Oct 15, 1894

I, Peter Clark, of Maurepas, La. who made Homestead Application No. 9590 for the S.E.1/4 of N.W.1/4. E ½ of S.W. ¼ of N.W. ¼ of Sec 2, T,9,S.R. 5 E former S.E. Dist of Miss River. Do hereby give notice of my intention to make final proof to establish my claim to the land above described, and that I expect to prove my residence and cultivation before Register and Receiver at New Orleans on December 10, 1894.

by two of the following witnesses:
Marshall Douglas, of all of Livingston Parish, La.
Charles Baptiste
Henry Tinkshell
Alfred Robinson
Robert Benefield
Ida T. Benefield
    his
Peter x Clark
    Mark
Land Office at New Orleans, La.

Oct. 17th, 1894

Notice of the above application will be published in the "Southland" printed at Maurepas, La., which I hereby designate as the newspaper published nearest the land described in said application.

G. McD. Brumby, Register

Notice to Claimant.—Give time and place of providing the name the title of the officer before whom proof is to be made; give names and post office address of four neighbors, two of whom must appear as your witness.

☙

Notice for Publication.

LAND OFFICE AT NEW ORLEANS, LA.,
October 17, 1894.

Notice is hereby given that the following named settler has filed notice of his intention to make final proof in support of his claim, and that said proof will be made before the Register or Receiver at New Orleans, La., on December 10, 1894, viz: Peter Clark, who made homestead entry No. 9590 for the southeast quarter of northwest quarter east half of southwest quarter and northwest quarter of southwest quarter Section 2, Township 9, south, Range 5, east, former southeast District east of Mississippi river.

He names the following witnesses to prove his continuous residence upon and cultivation of said land, viz.: Marshall Douglass, Charles Baptiste, Henry Tinkshell, Alfred Robinson, all of Livingston Parish, La.

G. McD. BRUMBY, Register.

The Southland (Maurepas, LA), October 17, 1894.

Notice for Publication

LAND OFFICE AT NEW ORLEANS, LA.,
October 17, 1894

Notice is hereby given that the following settler has filed notice of his intention to make final proof in support of his claim, and that said proof will be made before the Register of Receiver at New Orleans, La., on December 10, 1894, viz, Peter Clark, who made homestead entry No. 9590 for the southeast quarter of northwest quarter east half of southwest quarter and northwest quarter of southwest quarter Section 2, Township 9, south, Range 5, east former southeast District east of Mississippi river.

He names the following witnesses to prove his continuous residence upon and cultivation of said land, viz: Marshall Douglass, Charles Baptiste, Henry Tinkshell, Alfred Robinson, all of Livingston Parish, La.

G. McD. BRUMBY, Register

❧

CERTIFICATE AS TO POSTING OF NOTICE.
Land Office at New Orleans La.
Nov 11th, 1895

I, G. McD. Brumby, Register, do hereby certify that a notice, a printed copy of which is hereto attached, was by me posted in a conspicuous place in my office for a period of thirty days, I having first posted said notice on the 17th day of October, 1894.

G. McD. Brumby
Register
State of Louisiana
Parish of Livingston,

Personally appeared before me, F.F. Landry, as Notary Public, in and for the Parish of Livingston Robert Benefield who being duly sworn according to the law. Deposes that he is the Publisher of "The Southland" a Newspaper publisher at Maurepas, Parish of Livingston, La., and that the annexes notice of final Proof of Homestead settler, Peter Clark, was published in said "Southland" (6) six consecutive weeks as the law directs, to wit: Oct 31st, Nov 7, 14, 21,28, & Dec 5, 1894.

Robert R.W. Benefield

Sworn to 7 subscribed this the 6th day of December 1894
Frederick F. Landry
Notary Public
(insert newspaper clipping)

HOMESTEAD

LAND OFFICE at New Orleans La.
Nov 11, 1895
Final Certificate APPLICATION,
No. 5887No. 9590

It is hereby certified That, pursuant to the provisions of Section 2291, Revised Statutes of the United States, Peter Clark of Livingston Ph., has made payment in full for

S.E. ¼ OF N.W.1/4/
E1/2 OF S.W.1/4
& N.W.1/4 "S.W.1/4
& S.E. Dist. R of R of Section No. 2, in Township no 9 South, of Range No. 5 East, of the St. Helena Principal Meridian, containing 159 and 33/100 acres.

Now, therefore, be it known, That on presentation of this

Certificate to the Commissioner of the General Land Office, the said Peter Clark of Livingston Parish shall be entitled to a Patent for the Tract of Land described.

G. McD. Brumby
Register

﷼

(4-140.)

Final Receiver's Receipt No 5887   Application no 9590

HOMESTEAD.
Receiver's Office, New Orleans, LA.
Nov 11, 1895

Received of Peter Clark the sum of Five dollars--------------cents
Being the balance of payment required by law for the entry of -----

S.E. ¼ of NW ¼
E 1/2 of SW ¼
& NW ¼ SW ¼

Of Section 2 in Township 9, South, Range 5, east Range E.T. Holmer containing 159 33/100 acres, under Section 2291 of the Revised Statutes of the United States.
$5.00
Charles N. Johnston
Receiver.

$1.00 Testimony fee received. Number of written words, 680 Rate per 100 words 15

Appendix C
William B. Kemp vs. William Clark

413

William Clark vs. William B. Kemp
#1185
Parish of Livingston, Louisiana.
William B. Kemp William Clark
* * *

Whereas, I, Simpson H. Sharp, sheriff of the above said Parish and State and by virtue of an order to seize and sell issued out of the above said Court, in the above numbered and entitled cause, and in compliance with said order, I seized the property of the defendant, William Clark, described as follows:

All his undivided interest in and to the S. E. 1/2. of N.W. 1. ¼, E.1/2 of S. W. I/4   and N.W. ¼ of Section two (2). T.9.S.R.5.E, Southeastern District of Louisiana, in said Parish and State, containing One hounded and fifty-nine 33/100 acres (159.33).

And advertised the same in the Denham Springs News, a weekly newspaper published in said Parish for a period of more than 30 clear days, to sell the said property at the principal front door of the court house in the town of Centerville, said Parish and State, on Saturday October 26ᵗʰ, 1918, during legal sale hours of said day and on the said day of the sale, I repaired to the said court house door, and after having had the said property appraised and about the hours of one o'clock I first read the order of seizure and sale the advertisement In the said newspaper the mortgage certificate, from the clerk & hoarder and the oath of the appraisers and the appraisement of said property I then posted the property at public auction and invited the bid there on and after carrying the same, all being done in a clear audible distinct voice when Clinton Stegall bid for William B Kemp, the price and sum on One hundred and Fifty dollars, for the said interest of William Clark, in the property herein described, and the said bid being the last and highest bid received, and for two thirds of the said appraisement, I adjudicated the said interest of William B. Clark, in and to the property herein seized and described to the said William B. Kemp, for the said price and sum of One hundred and Fifty dollars, and the purchaser being the mortgage creditor herein, and the Plaintiff in said suit, I allowed him to retain in his hands the purchase. All being done according to law.

Now, therefore, in consideration of the premises, and the law in such case made and provided, I, do by those presents, grant, bargain, sell, assign, set over and deliver, unto William B Kemp, purchaser herein the said interest of William Clark, in and to the property herein named and described.

To have and to hold the same for his own free use and behalf forever,

In testimony whereof I have hereunto signed my name officially at my office, in Centerville, said Parish and State, on this 26ᵗʰ October 1916.

Witnesses:

<u>Clinton Stegall</u> <u>Simpson H. Sharp</u>
Sheriff of the Parish of Livingston, La
<u>Louis R. Kimball</u>

Truly Recorded in Sheriff's Dale Book "C" Page 124 & 125,
October 26, 1918
Simpson H. Sharp, Sheriff

(U.S. Documentary Stamps in the sum of 50c affixed and same are
duly cancelled)

Truly Recorded October 28th, 1918

<u>Louis R. Kimball</u>
Clerk and Recorder

Appendix D
Locations of Resources Used

Livingston Parish Clerk of Court 20180 Iowa Street Livingston, LA 70754	New Orleans Public Library, Genealogy Section 219 Loyola Avenue New Orleans, LA 70112
St. Helena Parish Clerk of Court 369 Sitman Street, #101 Greensburg, LA 70441	Amistad Research Center 6823 St Charles Avenue New Orleans, LA 70118
Livingston Parish Main Library 20390 Iowa Street Livingston, LA 70754	Tangipahoa Parish Library 204 NE Central Avenue Amite City, LA 70422
Louisiana State Archives 3851 Essen Lane Baton Rouge, LA 70809	Baton Rouge Main Public Library Genealogy Section Independence Park Library 7711 Goodwood Boulevard Baton Rouge, LA 70806
Goodwill Cemetery Maurepas, LA 70449	National Archives 700 Pennsylvania Avenue NW Washington, DC 20408
Mitchell Cemetery	Daughters of the American

30000 Mitchell Street Killian, LA 70454	Revolution, Library 1776 D Street NW Washington, DC 20006
Williams Research Center 410 Chartres Street New Orleans, LA 70130	Library of Congress 1776 D Street NW Washington, DC 20006
The Notarial Archives 1340 Poydras Street, Suite 360 New Orleans, LA 70112	Washington DC Family History Center 10000 Stoneybrook Drive Kensington, MD 20895

Appendix E
Brown vs. Heirs of Peter Clark

PARISH OF LIVINGSTON

STATE OF LOUISIANA

NO. 14,236   DIV.____

BARBARA DENDINGER BROWN

VS.

HEIRS OF PETER CLARK

FILED: _May 17, 1965_ DY. CLERK: _Artie Mae Cassan_

SUIT TO QUIET TAX TITLES

The petition of Barbara Dendinger Brown, a resident of

the Parish of Orleans, Louisiana, with respect shows:

1.

That petitioner, Barbara Dendinger Brown, is the sole and

only owner of the following described property in the Parish of

Livingston, Louisiana:

> The Southeast Quarter of the Northwest Quarter; the
> East Half of the Southwest Quarter; and the Northwest
> Quarter of the Southwest Quarter of Section 2, T9S.
> R5E, of the Southeastern Land District East of the
> Mississippi River, Parish of Livingston, State of
> Louisiana.

2.

That petitioner acquired said property from Theodore

Dendinger and others in accordance with deed dated April 16, 1956,

recorded in COB 79, page 276; that Theodore Dendinger and his co-

vendors acquired said property on April 2, 1956, as per COB 79,

page 169 from Dendinger, Inc.; that Dendinger, Inc. acquired said

property from Simpson H. Sharp and others on May 7, 1945, as per

COB 61, page 586; that Simpson H. Sharp acquired said property by

deeds recorded in COB 61, page 566 and COB 61, page 505 and COB 61,

That petitioner claims title by virtue of the aforementioned deeds and under the said tax deeds recorded in COB 39, page 309 and COB 40, page 314; that more than five years have elapsed since the registry of the above tax titles at the Clerk of Court's office in the Parish of Livingston, and petitioner, as sole owner of said property, desires to have the title thereto confirmed and quieted in accordance with Article 10, Section 11 of the Louisiana Constitution and Revised Statutes 47:2228.

4.

That neither the said Peter Clark or his heirs or legal representatives have been in possession of said property since the above tax sales, and it does not appear from the conveyance records that these parties have sold the property, or that same has been alienated in their name except for the above described tax sales.

5.

Petitioner does not know the whereabouts of the said Peter Clark or his heirs or legal representatives, and that it is necessary that a curator ad hoc be appointed in accordance with R.S. 47:2228.

WHEREFORE PETITIONER PRAYS that a curator ad hoc be appointed to represent the said defendant Peter Clark, his heirs, legal representatives or assigns; that said defendant be notified through the said curator ad hoc that title to the above described property will be confirmed and quieted unless a proceeding to annul the above described Tax Sales is instituted within ten days from date of service of the citation, petition and notice; that after due proceedings that there be Judgment in favor of petitioner

owner thereof in perfect ownership and forever enjoining and pro-
hibiting said defendant, his heirs and assigns from claiming or
setting up any right, title or interest to the said property or
any portion thereof; that should there be any difference between
the description of the property as appears hereinabove and the
Tax Deeds referred to herein, that the said Tax Deeds be reformed
to correspond to the property as described herein.

MENTZ & FORD

BY: /s/ T. Mentz

O R D E R.

Let   James M. Cudd   , attorney at law be
appointed curator ad hoc to represent and stand in judgment for
Peter Clark, his heirs, legal representatives or assigns and let
citation and notice issue herein as prayed for and according to
law.

Hammond, Louisiana, this 17th day of May, 1965.

DISTRICT JUDGE

STATE OF LOUISIANA

Barbara Dendinger Brown

14 236   VERSUS

Heirs of Peter Clark

21st JUDICIAL DISTRICT COURT

NO.

PARISH OF LIVINGSTON

TO THE DEFENDANT   James M. Cudd, curator of ad hoc

You are hereby summoned to comply with the demand contained in the petition of which a true and correct copy (exclusive of exhibits) accompanies this citation, or make an appearance, either by filing a pleading or otherwise, in the 21st Judicial District Court in and for the Parish of Livingston, State of Louisiana, within fifteen (15) days after the service hereof, under penalty of default.

Witness the Honorable the Judges of said Court this ____17th____ day of __MAY__

_____, A.D., 196_5_.

_____
Deputy Clerk of Court

SHERIFF'S PERSONAL RETURN

Received the within citation together with a copy thereof with certificate copy of petition thereto annexed on the __17__ day of __May_____, 19_65_, and on the __17__ day of __May_____ 19_65_, I served the aforesaid copy of within citation together with the certified copy of petition thereto attached, on _James M. Cudd_____ by handing the same to him in person.

Distance from the Court House ____0____ miles.

Service $__200__

Mi.   _____

_____
Sheriff

SHERIFF'S DOMICILIARY RETURN

Received the within citation together with a copy thereof with certified copy of petition thereto annexed on the _____ day of _____, 19_____, and on the _____ day of _____, 19_____. I served the aforesaid copy of within citation together with the certified copy of petition hereto attached, on _____

by leaving the same at his usual domicile in the Parish of Livingston in the hands of _____

a person apparently over 14 years of age, and living in the same house with the said _____

he being absent from home at the time of service. Distance from the Court House _____ miles.

Service $_____

Mi.   _____

_____
Sheriff

BARBARA DENDINGER BROWN

VS. NO. 14236

HEIRS OF PETER CLARK

FILED:_____

21ST JUDICIAL DISTRICT COURT

PARISH OF LIVINGSTON

STATE OF LOUISIANA

_____
DY. CLERK OF COURT

TRANSCRIPT of the notes of evidence taken in the above matter in Open Court
at Livingston , Louisiana this 11th day of __June__ 19 65
before His Honor, Warren W. Comish.
Representing Plaintiff: Mr. Leon Ford.
Representing Defendant: Mr. Jim Cudd, Attorney Ad Hoc.

- - -

This is a suit to quiet a Tax Title.

THEODORE J. DENDINGER, BEING DULY SWORN:

Q. State your full name please.

A. Theordore J. Dendinger.

Q. Mr. Dendinger, is Mrs. Barbara Dendinger Brown your daughter?

A. That is right.

Q. And she is the recognized owner of the property described in this
petition as SE¼ of NW¼, E½ of the SW¼, NW¼ of the SW¼ of Section
2, T9 SR 5E?

A. That is correct.

Q. Mr. Dendinger, she acquired this property from Dendinger, Inc.?

A. Right.

Q. What, if anything, is your connection with the Dendinger, Inc.?

A. I worked as Assistant Manager at that time.

Q. When did Dendinger, Inc. acquire this property?

A. In 1945.

Q. And when was it 1956 approximately when she acquired it from
Dendinger?

A. Yes, in the Liquidation of Dendinger, Inc.

Q. Mr. Dendinger, you were acquainted with the ownership and possession
of it while it was owned by Dendinger, Inc. and during the time it was
owned by your daughter?

A. Yes sir.

Q. Has there ever been any question about the ownership or possession
of this property?

A. No, we cut timber on it 1948, latter part of '48 and early part of

120

'49. The corporation did. Then my daughter has cut timber on it.

BY MR. FORD:

Your Honor, at this time I would like to offer in evidence
the deed dated April 16th, 1956 recorded in COB 79, Page 276, Parish of
Livingston; the deed dated April 2nd, 1956, COB 79, Page 169, Parish of
Livingston, both of those deeds from Dendinger, Inc. to Barbara
Dendinger Brown; deed dated May 7th, 1945 in COB 61, Page 586 from
Simpson H. Sharp to Dendinger, Inc.; and deed dated--rather the deeds
in COB 61, Page 566; COB 61, Page 505; COB 61, Page 515; COB 45, Page
611 with reference to the Estate of Vivian E.Settoon and the two tax
sales involved in COB 40, Page 314 and COB 39, Page 309. Ask leave
to submit certified or photostatic copies. That is 1923 and 1924
Tax Sale.

Also offer at this time a copy of an affidavit of
Steve Lauzeruich and Roy Lauzervich with reference to the possession of
this tract. And ask leave to substitute a copy of this affidavit.

BY MR. CUDD:

If the Court please, I was appointed Curator to represent
Peter Clark, Tax Debtor and I made inquiries about the Courthouse and
nobody seemed to know him. I checked the assessment roll in the Fifth
Ward and he is not assessed with any property. I checked with Mrs.
Sibley, Voter Registrar and he was not registered . I learned later
that he had been dead for quite some time. I also checked the indices
of the Conveyance Records and I found no sales of the property to
Peter Clark, in fact the only two sales in his name that appear in the
indices are the two tax sales.

BY THE COURT:

Q. Did you check the Succession Records?

A. Yes sir. The only acts that I found in his name is the conveyance
of the two tax sales.

Q. There was no succession recorded?

A. No sir.

--

121

TWENTY-FIRST JUDICIAL DISTRICT COURT

PARISH OF LIVINGSTON

STATE OF LOUISIANA

NO. 14,236   DIV. "A"

BARBARA DENDINGER BROWN

VS.

HEIRS OF PETER CLARK

FILED:_____DY. CLERK:_____

J U D G M E N T

    This cause came on for trial, pursuant to regular assignment, was duly tried and submitted, and the law and the evidence being in favor of plaintiff and against defendants, for the oral reasons assigned:

    IT IS ORDERED, ADJUDGED AND DECREED that petitioner, Barbara Dendinger Brown, have judgment in her favor and against defendant, Peter Clark, his heirs, legal representatives, or assigns, confirming and quieting the tax deeds recorded in COB 39, page 309 and COB 40, page 314, and recognizing the title of petitioner as the sole and only owner of the following described property:

        The SE/4 of NW/4; E/2 of SW/4; and NW/4 of SW/4 of
        Section 2, T9S, R5E, Livingston Parish, Louisiana.

    IT IS FURTHER ORDERED, ADJUDGED AND DECREED that defendant, Peter Clark, his heirs, legal representatives, or assigns, be forever enjoined and prohibited from claiming or setting up any right, title or interest in and to the above described property or any portion thereof; and that should there be any difference between the description of property as appears hereinabove and the tax deeds referred to herein, that said tax deeds be, and the same are hereby reformed to correspond to the property as above described.

    JUDGMENT RENDERED, READ AND SIGNED in open Court at Livingston, Louisiana, on this 11th day of June, 1965.

                                     _____

MENTZ & FORD   DISTRICT JUDGE

BY:_____
    Attorneys for Petitioner

VS. NO. 14,250

HEIRS OF PETER CLARK   : STATE OF LOUISIANA

- - - - - - - - - - - - - - :- - - - - - - - - - - - - - -

ANSWER

Now, into Court, comes James M. Cudd, Attorney at
Law, appointed curator ad hoc to represent the absentees, Peter
Clark and/or his heirs, made defendants herein, and for answer to
plaintiff's petition, says;

1

That for lack of sufficient information to justify
a belief, respondent denies, all and singular, the allegations
of plaintiff's petition.

2

Your respondent submits the matter to the Court
and asks that plaintiff be held to strict proof of her demand.

WHEREFORE, respondent prays that this answer be
considered full and sufficient; that the same be filed herein,
and that, after proceedings had herein, there be judgment dis-
missing the plaintiff's demand at her expense.

And for general and equitable relief in the
premises.

         _____
        James M. Cudd, Curator ad hoc.

[Transcription]

State of Louisiana:
Parish of Livingston:

Before me, the undersigned authority, personally came and appeared STEVE LAUZERVICH and ROY LAUZERVICH, who after being duly sworn by me, depose and say:

That they are residents of Maurepas, Livingston Parish, Louisiana, and that they are familiar with the following described property to-wit;

The Southeast Quarter of the Northwest Quarter, the East Half of the Southwest Quarter, and the Northwest Quarter of the Southwest Quarter of Section 2, Township 9 South, Range 5 East, Greensburg Land District, containing 159.33 acres, more or less, and being in Livingston Parish, Louisiana.

Affiants further depose and say

That the caption land is all wooded and about one-half highland and the remainder in the tidewater swamp.

That about 60 years ago Peter Clark, colored, was living on the tract with his family. Improvements consisted of a dwelling house and other farm buildings. About 30 acres of the tract was fenced and cultivated by Clark until his death about 45 years ago. Some of his family lived on the North portion of the land for several years, the last persons moving off of the property about 40 years ago with all improvements disappeared through neglect. Since that time there have been no improvements on the land and none of the land has been enclosed by a fence

The tract was brought in for taxes by Simpson Sharp about 35 years ago and sold to the Dendinger Company about 25years ago. About 15 or 20 years ago the tract was surveyed by Y.A. Tycer (sic) Surveyor for the Dendinger Company. At that time the lines around the tract were well marked with (illegible) and those lines can still be located at the present time. The survey did not encroach on any of the adjoining property owners.

About 15 or 20 years ago the Dendinger Company cut timber all over the tract, working the land for several months. About 7 or 8 years ago the present owner Barbara Dendinger Brown, had some pine timber cut on the highland portion of the land.

That to the best of the affiants knowledge and belief, the present owner of the caption land, Barbara Dendinger Brown and her predecessors in title have enjoyed opened and peaceable and continuous possession of the caption land for more than 50 years and we have never known of any adverse claims or any encroachment by adjoining property owners.

Witnesses   Steve Lauzervich
 L.B. Kinchen

                                            Roy Lauzervich

(Illegible)

Sworn to and subscribe before 17 May 196(sic)

_____
Notary Public and for
Livingston Parish, Louisiana

Sheriff and Ex-Officio Tax Collector, as aforesaid, acting under the authority vested in me by law, do hereby grant, bargain, sell, convey, set over and deliver unto L L POWERS, purchaser aforesaid, in and to the property heretofore adjudicated, together with all the rights and actions which the said A S CORNET, tax debtor, had in and to the same.

It being and understood however, that in conformity with law, the said Tax debtor may redeem the same at any time with one year after day of sale, by paying the said purchaser the amount of the total tax, interest and costs, together with twenty per cent added thereto.

In witness whereof, I have signed these presents at my office at Springville Livingston Parish, Louisiana, on this the 20th, day of June 1925, in the presence of the two competent witnesses.

Clinton Stegall.
Vivian E Settoon,

EDGAR P GUITREAU,
Dy, Sheriff and Ex-Officio Tax-
Officio Tax Collector Parish
of Livingston, La.

Filed for Record June 23rd, 1925.
Recorded June23rd, 1925.

20128 A

Clerk & Recorder,

....
: PETER CLARK.   :
:   TO   :
: V. E. SETTOON. :
....

STATE OF LOUISIANA
PARISH OF LIVINGSTON.

WHEREAS, I, Edgar P Guitreau, Deputy Sheriff under Louis R Kimball, Sheriff and Ex-Officio Tax-Collector, within and for the Parish of Livingston, State of Louisiana, by the authority vested in me by the Constitution and laws of the State of Louisiana, and in accordance with Act 170 of the General Assembly of 1898 and all laws amendatort thereto

And having made the necessary publication and advertisement, to-wit: In the Denham Springs News, a newspaper published weekly in the town of Denham Springs, Parish of Livingston, Louisiana, said publication being completed on the 18th, day of June 1925, and having complied with all the formalities required and specified in said acts, did seize and expose at public auction, on the 20th, day of June 1925, at the Courthouse door, in the town of Centerville (Springville Postoffice) Parish of Livingston, State of Louisiana, the following described property, situated in said Parish and State, to-wit;

160 acres; SE¼ of NW¼, E½ of SW¼, & NW¼ of SE¼, Sec.2,T.9,S.R.5.E.,

The same having been seized for the payment of the taxes due by Peter Clark, according to tableau and assessment for the year 1924, at which sale V E Settoon, bid the whole of said property, and this being the last and highest bid received and for the least portion of said property, the said property was adjudicated to the said V E Settoon, his heirs and assigns, for the sum of Sixty & 25/100 Dollars as follows.

State tax, ...	$ 8.40.
Parish Tax, ...	6.40
6Mill Parish Wide School.	8.00
3, Mill Constitutiona School.	4.80
Road District NO. 3.	10.40
Road District NO.3.	8.00
Road District.NO.3.,.v..	4.80
Tick Eradication.	1.60
Interest.	1.60
Notice.	.25
Printer's Bill	3.00
Deed.	1.50
Recorder's fee.	1.50
Total	$60.25.

NOW THEREFORE, I, Edgar P Guitreau, Deputy Sheriff under Louis R Kimball, Sheriff and Ex-Officio Tax Collector, as aforesaid, acting under the authority vested in me by law, do hereby grant, bargain, sell, convey, set over and deliver unto V E Settoon, purchaser aforesaid, in and to the property heretofore adjudicated, together with all rights and actions which the said Peter Clark, tax debtor, had in and to the same.

It being and understood however; that in conformity with law, the said tax debtor may redeem the same at any time within one year after day of sale, by paying the said purchaser the amount of the total tax, interest and costs, together with twenty per cent added thereto.

IN WITNESS WHEREOF, I have signed these presents at my office at Springville Livingston Parish, Louisiana, on this, the 20th day of June in the presence of the two competent witnesses.

Clinton Stegall.
Vivian E Settoon.

Edgar P Guitreau
Dy, Sheriff and Ex-Officio Tax Collector
Livingston Parish, La.

Filed for Record June 23rd, 1925.
Recorded June 23rd, 1925.

Clerk & Recorder.

kind or description, including claims of collation and Federal and State Tax claims or liens, arising or to arise out of the estate of the late Theodore Dendinger.

THUS EXECUTED on this 17th day of June, 1965, at New Orleans, Louisiana, in the presence of the undersigned competent witnesses and me, Notary, after due reading of the whole.

WITNESSES:

Dorothy Futavy

Lorraine Schmaltz

Mrs. Anna Davenport Dendinger
MRS. ANNA DAVENPORT DENDINGER

Mrs. Anna Joyce Dietz Dendinger
MRS. ANNA JOYCE DIETZ DENDINGER

Evelyn Dendinger Walton
MRS. EVELYN DENDINGER WALTON

Roy F. Mentz
NOTARY PUBLIC

CASH DEED   3. Copies
★

BARBARA DENDINGER BROWN

TO

CROWN ZELLERBACH CORPORATION

STATE OF LOUISIANA
PARISH OF TANGIPAHOA

No. 54926

Filed 3:10 P.M. July 26, 65

Wayne Strain
DY. CLERK OF COURT

BEFORE ME,   HENRY A. MENTZ, JR.,   a Notary Public, duly commissioned and qualified, in and for the Parish of Tangipahoa, State of Louisiana, and in the presence of the witnesses hereinafter named and undersigned, personally came and appeared

BARBARA DENDINGER BROWN, once married and then to Bobby Brown, with whom she is living, a resident of Orleans Parish, Louisiana,

who declared that, for and in consideration of the price of and sum of
SIXTEEN THOUSAND AND NO/100 - - - - - - - - - - - - - - - -DOLLARS ($16,000.00) cash in hand paid, the receipt of which is hereby acknowledged and good acquittance and discharge given for the same,   she   did and does by these presents grant, bargain, sell, convey, assign, set over, and deliver unto

CROWN ZELLERBACH CORPORATION, a Nevada corporation with its principal office at No. One Bush Street, City of San Francisco, California, and its Louisiana domicile in the City of Bogalusa,

here present, accepting, and purchasing for   itself   , its   heirs, successors, and assigns, all and singular, the following described property, to-wit:

160 acres of land, more or less, in Section 2, T9S, R5E, Livingston Parish, Louisiana, being the Southeast Quarter of Northwest Quarter (SE/4 of NW/4); the East Half of Southwest Quarter (E/2 of SW/4) and the Northwest Quarter of Southwest Quarter (NW/4 of SW/4), all as per survey annexed hereto, dated July, 1965, prepared by John W. Kellan, Jr..

The vendor reserved to herself, her heirs and assigns, one half of all mineral rights in and to the above described property.

31826

RECORDED THURSDAY, JULY 29, 1965

113 / 824

127

To have and to hold the above described property   and all appurtenances   unto the said
Purchaser   its   heirs, successors, and assigns, in full property forever, free from any lien, mortgage, privilege, or encumbrance whatsoever, with full and general warranty of title, and with full subrogation to all
rights of warranty and other rights as held therein by said vendor.

The certificate required by Article 3264 of the Revised Civil Code of this State is waived by the parties, who
agree to hold me, Notary, harmless for the non-production thereof.

All taxes on the above described property for the three years preceeding passage of this Act have been paid as
evidenced by the attached certificates, and the parties agree that taxes for the current year are pro-rated.

Thus Done, Signed, and Passed at my office in ....Hammond.... , in the Parish of Tangipahoa, State of
Louisiana, this 10th day of   July   19 65 in the presence of   Constance V. Berry

and   Lois J. Schilling   competent witnesses, who signed these presents with said
appearers and Me, said Notary, after due reading of the whole.

WITNESSES

Constance V. Berry
Constance V. Berry

Barbara Dandinger Brown
Barbara Dandinger Brown
Bobby Brown

Lois J. Schilling
Lois J. Schilling

Henry A. Mentz Jr.
HENRY A. MENTZ, JR. NOTARY PUBLIC

RECORDED _____ 19 ____
IN CONVEYANCE BOOK _____
PAGE _____ OF THE OFFICIAL RECORDS
OF TANGIPAHOA PARISH, LA.

DY. CLERK & RECORDER

RECORDED THURSDAY, JULY 29, 1965

128.

Taxes for the current year (have been) (will be) paid in the proportion of **pro-rata** by SELLER.
All parties signing the within instrument have declared themselves to be of full legal capacity.

All agreements and stipulations herein, and all the obligations herein assumed shall inure to the benefit of and be binding upon the heirs, successors, and assigns of the respective parties, and the BUYER, his heirs and assigns shall have and hold the described property in full ownership forever.

The certificate of mortgages required by Article 3361 of the Revised Civil Code of Louisiana is dispensed with by the parties. Certificates are annexed showing that taxes assessed against the property have been paid. U. S. Internal Revenue stamps are affixed in the amount of $ 0.55

Done and signed by the parties at my office in Denham Springs the date first above written, in the presence of me, Notary, and the following competent witnesses who have signed in the presence of the parties and me, Notary.

Witnesses:

_____   _____
DARLENE SCIENK   MRS. BEATRICE McMORRIS

_____   _____
MILDRED DURBIN   JERRY C. BOND

_____
ERLO J. DURBIN   Notary Public

CASH DEED
★

	STATE OF LOUISIANA
Alfred B. Sibley	PARISH OF LIVINGSTON
TO	No. 63489
Gayle O. Hill	Filed at 2:10 P.M. on July 19, 1967
	Dy. Clerk of Court

BEFORE ME, Hobart O. Pardue, Jr. , a Notary Public, duly commissioned and qualified, in and for the Parish of Livingston, State of Louisiana, and in the presence of the witnesses hereinafter named and undersigned, personally, came and appeared

Alfred B. Sibley, married to and living with Winnie St. Amant, residents of the Parish of Livingston, State of Louisiana.

who declared that, for and in consideration of the price of and sum of FOUR THOUSAND EIGHT HUNDRED FIFTY-FIVE AND 50/100-- DOLLARS ($4855.50) cash in hand paid, the receipt of which is hereby acknowledged and good acquittance and discharge given for the same, did and do by these presents grant, bargain, sell, convey, assign, set over, and deliver, unto

Gayle O. Hill, married to and living with Irene Upwald, residents of El Paso County, Colorado.

here, present, accepting, and purchasing for their heirs, successors, and assigns, all and singular, the following described property, to-wit:

Commence at Northeast Corner Section 51; run South 60 chains to Point of Beginning or starting point...Thence run West 4.00 chains to South margin of road; thence along road South 77¼° West 0.49 chains; thence South 0° 45 minutes West 10.50 chains; thence South 2° 20 minutes West 5.21 chains; thence North 89° 30 minutes East 12.37 chains; thence North 0° 30 minutes West 21.00 chains to South margin of road; Thence along road South 62½° West 8.44 chains; thence South 1.28 chains to Point of Beginning containing 11.58 acres being located in Section 27, Township 8 South, Range 6 East, Livingston Parish, Louisiana; according to a map by C. M. Moore, Civil Engineer and Surveyor, dated November 23, 1959.

63489

129

To have and to hold the above described property   unto the said
Purchaser   their   heirs, successors, and assigns, in full property forever, free from any lien, mortgage, privilege, or encumbrance whatsoever, with full and general warranty of title, and with full subrogation to all rights of warranty and other rights as held therein by said vendor.

The certificate required by Article 3564 of the Revised Civil Code of this State is waived by the parties, who agree to hold me, Notary, harmless for the non-production thereof.

All taxes on the above described property for the three years preceding passage of this Act have been paid as evidenced by the attached certificates, and the parties agree that taxes for the current year are

Thus Done, Signed, and Passed at my office in   Springfield   , in the Parish of Livingston, State of Louisiana, this 13th day of July   1967 , in the presence of   Winnie S. Sibley

And L. E. Barton Sr.   competent witnesses, who signed these presents with said appearers and Me, said Notary, after due reading of the whole.

WITNESSES

Winnie S. Sibley   _Alfred B. Cooley_

L. E. Barton Jr.

(signature)
NOTARY PUBLIC

RECORDED _____ 19____
IN CONVEYANCE BOOK _____
PAGE _____ OF THE OFFICIAL RECORDS
OF LIVINGSTON PARISH, LA.

_____
DY. CLERK & RECORDER

130

Bibliography

- "$300.00 Reward," *Daily Advocate* (Baton Rouge, LA), April 20, 1886, p.4
- Blassingame, John W. *Black New Orleans, 1860-1880*. Chicago: The University of Chicago Press, 1973.
- Edward Livingston Historical Association, History Book Committee, ed. *History of Livingston Parish, Louisiana, 1986*. Dallas, Tex.: Curtis Media Corp., c1986.
- Hair, William Ivy. *Bourbonism and Agrarian Protest: Louisiana Politics, 1877-1900*. Baton Rouge: Louisiana State University Free Press, 1969.
- Hawkins, Kenneth. *Research in the Land Entry files of the General Land Office-Record Group 49, Reference Information Paper 114. Revised.* Washington, D.C.: National Archives and Records Administration, 2009.
- *Herringshaw's Encyclopedia of American Biography of the Nineteenth Century.* Chicago, IL: American Publishers' Association, 1898.
- Hyde, Samuel C. *Pistols and Politics: The Dilemma of Democracy in Louisiana, 1810-1899*. Baton Rouge: Louisiana State University Free Press, 1996.
- "Leading the Way: Walter Louis Cohen." *New Orleans Tribune.* 2017. [website] http://www.theneworleanstribune.com/main/leading-the-way-walter-louis-cohen/

- "Murder in Livingston Parish," *Maurepas (LA) Gazette*, Reported in the *Daily Advocate* (Baton Rouge, LA), March 18, 1884, p.4.
- "Not the Man," *Donaldsonville (LA) Chief*, April 10, 1886, p.4.
- Oubre, Claude F. "Forty Acres and a Mule: Louisiana and the Southern Homestead Act." *Louisiana History: The Journal of the Louisiana of the Louisiana Historical Association*, Vol. 17. No. 2 (Spring, 1976), pp. 143-157.
- Painter, Nell Irvin. *Exodusters; Black Migration to Kansas After Reconstruction*. New York: W.W. Norton, 1986.
- Pardue, D. N. "Biography of Pierre Etienne LeBourgeois, Livingston, St. James and Orleans Parishes, Louisiana." *French Settlement Historical Register*, vol. 5 (December 1980). French Historical Society. http://files.usgwarchives.net/la/orleans/bios/l-000014.txt.
- Poret, Ory G. *History of Land Titles in the State of Louisiana*. Baton Rouge: State of Louisiana, Division of Administration, State Land Office, 1972.
- *Records of the Field Offices for the State of Louisiana, Bureau of Refugees, Freedmen, and Abandoned Lands, 1863-1872. Record Group 105*. Washington, D.C.: National Archives and Records Administration.
- USDA. "Black Farmers in America, 1865-2000: The Pursuit of Independent Farming and the Role of Cooperatives." *RBS Research Report 194*.
- Vincent, Charles, ed. "The African American Experience In Louisiana: Part B: From the Civil War to Jim Crow" in *The Louisiana Purchase Bicentennial Series in Louisiana History, Volume 9*. Lafayette: Center for Louisiana Studies, University of Louisiana at Lafayette, 2000.
- "Was Homesteading Only For White People?" (July 7, 2011) Friends of Homestead National Monument of America. [website] http://homesteadcongress.blogspot.com/2011/07/was-homesteading-only-for-white-people.html

Index

Quinn, Hester Clark Robinson, 58, 77, 99; education, 58; New Orleans, 57
Rienzi Plantation (Lafourche Parish (LA)), 71
Robinson, Alfred, 83, 85, 89
Robinson, Minerva, 62
Rousseau, S., 90
Russell, Clovice, 91
Sharp, Simpson H., 94-95
Skinner, Henry, 56
Smiley, John, 90
Smith, John, 90
Smith, Leonard, 70
Southland and Gazette (Maurepas, LA), 88
St. Helena Parish (LA), 21, 60, 73-74; courthouse, 61
St. Tammany Parish (LA), 57
Stegall, Clinton, 94
Thomy Lafon Elementary School (New Orleans), 40
Tiger Bluff Baptist Church, 56
Tiger Bluff Baptist Church School, 44
Tillery, William H., 62, 74
Tinkshell, Corinne, 87
Tinkshell, Henry N., 83-87, 90, 92
United States Colored Cavalry, 86
United States Colored Troops, 88, 91
Vidal, Adriene, see Vidal Gumersindo Adriene

Vidal, Delphine Baptiste, 83, 91
Vidal, Gumersindo Adriene, 88, 90-91
Watson Family Reunion, 99
Watson, Berlin, 48; birth, 30; death, 56
Watson, Henry Ernest, xvi, 22, 55
Watson, Rebecca, see Mitchell, Rebecca Watson
Webb, R.C., 72
Webber, Sandford, 89
Whitehall (LA), see Maurepas (LA)
Youngblood, Charles, 64
Youngblood, Charley, 50
Youngblood, Dave, 64
Youngblood, Henry, 64
Youngblood, Lewis, 50, 64-68; murder, 50
Youngblood, Marshall, 64
Youngblood, Minerva Smith, xv, 62, 64, 66, 99; marriage bond, 61
Youngblood, Monroe, 52, 64
Youngblood, Pink, 64
Youngblood, Rebecca, see Clark, Rebecca Youngblood
Youngblood, Roda Ann, 64
Youngblood, Thomas, xv, 63-64, 74, 84, 87, 88, 99; estate, 65-68, 91; marriage bond, 61
Youngblood, Thomas Jr., 50-52, 64, 67
Youngblood, William, 64

Made in the USA
Middletown, DE
16 March 2019